LET GO AND
LIVE IN THE
N☀W

LET GO AND LIVE IN THE NW

Awaken the Peace, Power, and Happiness in Your Heart

By the best-selling author of
The Secret of Letting Go

GUY FINLEY

Red Wheel
Boston, MA / York Beach, ME

First published in 2004 by
Red Wheel/Weiser, LLC
York Beach, ME
With offices at:
368 Congress Street
Boston, MA 02210
www.redwheelweiser.com

Library of Congress Cataloging-in-Publication Data
Finley, Guy.
  Let go and live in the now : awaken the peace, power, and
happiness in your heart / Guy Finley.
      p. cm.
  Includes bibliographical references.
  ISBN 1-59003-070-2
  1. Self-actualization (Psychology) I. Title.
  BF637.S4.F555 2004
  158.1--dc22

                              2004011360

Typeset in Novarese Book by Garrett Brown
Printed in Canada
TCP

11 10 09 08 07 06 05 04
 8 7 6 5 4 3 2 1

To Patricia, my wife, my heart, my friend, my life's editor-at-large, my confidant, and my love. Thanks to you for always being there to help me see where there was further yet to go. This book is better because of you.

TABLE OF CONTENTS

CONTENTS

CONTENTS

WHAT IS THIS
BOOK ALL ABOUT?

Just as bridges must be built between cultures and countries, so too must bridges be built to span the distance between the great wisdom teachings of centuries past and our own times. *Let Go and Live in the Now* is such a bridge. Its gentle but sometimes shocking revelations reach right into the mind of the seeker of the higher life, filling it with a palpable new light that helps bridge the distance between who we are at present and what we may yet become.

Each chapter is filled with timeless principles presented in a current context. These principles are made practical and are empowered by the numerous ways in which the author suggests their application to modern-day life. Much more than just a set of "how to" instructions, this is a book whose thought-provoking stories and penetrating insights work directly upon the heart of the reader, to help start the internal process of self-healing.

Let Go and Live in the Now is a living example of the timeless wholeness to which it leads its reader. It is gentle and striking, urgent and restive, serious and light-hearted. This book is for any person who longs not just to discover the truth of themselves, but who wishes to become a conscious participant in the great transformation of our Living Universe.

INTRODUCTION

Making Friends with the Mystery of Ourselves

Here is a simple truth that deserves our special attention: A *life without mystery in it isn't a real life at all*. In fact, this seldom-considered truth about what enriches our lives and makes them worthwhile is *itself* a mystery that deserves our thought. To get started, we need only return to the days of our youth.

Can we remember when, in those more tender years—before our sense of wonder was either crushed, or brushed away by a world rushing by—how alive we were with a bare longing *to know life by itself*? How life's mysteries held no fear for us, but rather filled us with expectations . . . so much so that some nights it was hard to fall asleep; or we'd spend the night actively dreaming of all of the possibilities life seemed to offer? Can we look back on ourselves when we were like this and recall when our hearts and minds were still wide open; how intrigued we were by the world unfolding around us, even as we were awakening to an exploding universe of feelings welling up within us?

Remember that deep fascination we felt toward our dearest friends, male and female alike; how we were so drawn to some that we couldn't spend enough time together? We expressed our affections to those closest to us with no regard for how we might be perceived. And then, of course, there were the *others* in our lives—those people for whom we felt close to nothing at all, and about whom we silently wondered what possible purpose was being served by their existence on earth!

And who can forget that strange fascination with the surging sensation of inconsolable crying when someone broke our hearts for the first time? Or that pain (or pleasure) of wanting someone, or something, so much that it felt like we couldn't breathe? Everything was vital: one moment driven by a new desire, the next moment all but dead to it. On and on it went, and that was all right. . . . Growing up was tied together by a string of enigmas like these. Our days were like a string of pearls of different colors and sizes, where our new answers to life only introduced us to still newer questions! But back *then* our urgency to resolve these uncertainties was nothing like it seems today. Somehow we knew, in spite of our youth, that *the true nature of mysteries is for one to replace another* and so letting go came naturally.

Even so, as we would all come to realize in the fullness of time, these early life mysteries of ours *were only a herald of things to come*. Each, it would turn out, was but a small piece of a much older, far greater puzzle—one whose presence went with us everywhere but whose grand and invisible character, like the sky that surrounds us, was just too big for us to see. But we were children then, with childish understanding. Now we must understand anew.

It turns out this grand or *central* mystery around whose corners we danced as kids remains the spice of life, lending a special savor to all of our questions about life. Without the continuing presence of this grand mystery in our lives all of the *lesser* mysteries that come our way would be as meaningless as characters in a story without a central figure that defines their reason for being.

So then what is this central mystery, this secret sun in the system of ourselves, around which all our relationships revolve and which shines light on their very purpose for being? Here is the answer: It *is the mystery of Self.*

Self . . . that imperceptible but ever-present center within us from which we watch life dance around us, bringing us what it will and from where it wills, an intimate place in each of us from where—each time the music suddenly stops and the stage goes empty—we stand there, silently wondering to ourselves: "*Who am* I and *what was that all about?*"

To one degree or another, regardless of causes past or present, all of us are familiar with these silent promptings to search out the truth of ourselves, to uncover the hidden reason for our being who and what we are. But within these silent urgings *there dwells an unseen mystery*. After all, why should life stir any of us, as it does, to ponder the hidden nature of our own self? What profit is there in troubling ourselves over something so unseen and unproven as that—particularly when it seems a given that all we need to be happy *has already been provided* for us in the visible world. As the mythic detective Sherlock Holmes surely would have told his trusted sidekick when observing these clues, "Elementary, my dear Watson;" this search for our unseen self can have but one cause: *We are not content with ourselves as we are.*"

And when all is said and done, isn't this strange "hole" in the center of our soul—this unhappiness that we can't find an answer for, nor explain away—the *real* mystery? Especially given the fact that no matter what we do to please ourselves—from winning some new success to jumping into a "better" relationship to ease an old bitterness in our hearts—nothing really works. The best we achieve for our efforts is a temporary abeyance of an emptiness that returns to prove itself greater than our power to push it away.

The fact is that this discontent with Self runs through the fiber of our soul as the strains of a dark melody run through a song written in a minor key. By degrees and in diverse moments, we all feel the strain of it coursing through us, set into motion by some unseen timetable of passing events. We have all felt that empty feeling come to fill us when our former passion for someone, or something, inexplicably begins to wane, or in those too-silent moments following some grand achievement of ours—when we look out upon the now naked land-scape of our own future and see, once again, it needs replanting.

It is in these unwanted times when we are so close to the forest that *we can't see the trees*. We are literally blinded—either by not want-ing to see the approaching shadows of our own fading happiness—or by the self-induced brilliance of our latest plan to replace the one aging before our eyes. And it is because of this, our lost "sight," that we miss seeing the great mystery behind what life has been trying to show us all along!

If our continuing sense of discontentment within ourselves, and with this life, were *earthly* in nature then certainly *our sense of emptiness would have an earthly solution*; but as we have proven to ourselves time and time again, it does not. And that's just the point. Now can we begin to see how gently this realization whispers to us of a mystery that begins in one world and leads us to another?

The discontentment with our life has its origin in the U*nseen*, in what is supernal. And as surprising as it may seem at first, the facts stand clear: this grand mystery that runs through our lives has been inviting us to seek a spiritual solution to our sufferings. Can you see how this insight changes everything about our search to solve the mystery of the Hidden Self? Not only are we in need of higher answers to help us discern its True Nature, but we also need a whole new set of questions to help us do the interior work of uncovering it!

Above all, one thing should be self-evident: a *cover-up* of some kind must be taking place within us! After all, what could be nearer to us than our own True Nature? Yet it lies undiscovered! And this key revelation—that something is interfering with our wish to realize the truth of ourselves—begs us to ask this one great question of ourselves, one of many that we will solve together as we grow in new self-understanding: *What are these unseen forces that are at work within us and that want to keep us from realizing a relationship with our own secret heart? What must we do to realize the hidden power, promise, and freedom that awaits us in our own Higher Self?*

In this book you will discover more than just the answers to these mysteries hidden within your present Self. You will meet an indwelling True Self that never runs from anything because this Higher Nature knows that what is endless need never fear anything that changes in passing time. You will learn how to say "No" to a host of negative thoughts and feelings, and discover how you can turn any moment of darkness into a guiding light. And most important of all, you will make fast friends with timeless truths. You will meet dozens and dozens of bright, light-filled, eternal principles in whose cheerful company you will be safely guided all the way back home to the true and hidden you.

One last thought before we take our journey together: Embrace all of the mysteries about yourself that you will meet along the way; in fact, learn to welcome them with open arms. See that each mystery about our Hidden Self is the same as its promise to us; it is life's silent pledge, a divine promise that we stand on the threshold of an ever higher, more complete understanding. It is we who are enlarged by our own self-discovery, for the eternal truth of any mystery is always, at last, found only within ourselves.

CHAPTER ONE

To Heal the Hidden Heart of You

There are so many wonderful mysteries not only in this world through which we journey but also right within each of us! For instance, did you know that the distance from your heart to your toes is, proportionally, approximately the same distance as our sun to the most distant planet in the solar system? And did you know that all creatures—from the common garden gnat to the great whales that swim the seas—all have roughly the same number of heartbeats in a lifetime? What a mystery is this heart whose character we share; how unfathomable, how attractive, how powerful, how potentially perfect is its undiscovered promise.

But down through the ages the Wise have spoken of a still deeper mystery. Great prophets and sages alike have long taught that this heart hidden in the center of us—our own physical heart—is but a three-dimensional reflection of an invisible Celestial Heart whose outpouring life secretly animates our own. Imagine something like a water drop shot out from the spray of a huge coastal breaker—complete in itself with all the qualities and capabilities of water, and yet only a microcosmic version of the timeless ocean from which it springs and to which it returns—and you'll have some idea of this wondrous vision.

If this description of the heart strikes you as being majestic, tireless, and timelessly magical, that's because it is just that! And in some ways each of us knows this heritage to be true. Each time we intuit our native home to be among the unmeasured stars, or sense within us a vitality and capacity to give from resources without end, we have felt the beating of this Real Heart that dwells within our Hidden Self. And strangely enough, as we will see in the pages that follow, it is this vast potential that we feel beating in us that often makes our present state of Self seem so unsatisfactory, a captive of our own unrealized possibilities.

EIGHT INDICATIONS OF A BROKEN HEART

Katie was a bright young woman who knew something wasn't quite right with her life. She also knew that she didn't have a clue what her sense of discontentment was about. After all, the Fates had been relatively kind to her, or so her friends had always said. That's what made her state so confounding. In the truest sense of the words she had "been there and done that," but in the end she remained as she began—unable to resolve a nagging sense of disappointment with herself and with life.

And so, not knowing what else to do, even beginning to wonder if perhaps her problem might have some physical cause, she decided to call upon the family doctor, an elderly man who not only took care of her as a child, but who had also watched over her parents while they were alive. Katie trusted him and his judgment; she knew that he would be able to help her. With one quick call, she scheduled her appointment for the following day.

Walking into the doctor's small office that sat tucked in the back corner of his modest home, Katie was flooded with memories of what felt like better days gone by. Not much had changed; there was still an old candy jar sitting on the faded cabinet, where equally faded-looking instruments rested in small metal trays. A moment later, she began to wonder if this visit was a mistake but it was too late to change her mind; the doctor walked in and his warm smile washed away all her concerns. "Hello, Katie," he said. "I haven't seen you in such a long time. What brings you here today?"

Suddenly she felt silly, and he must have sensed this because he interrupted her: "Come on," he teased, "Let's have it. Nothing can be that bad!" His simple manner overcame her self-consciousness and almost in a gush she told him about the sense of dead weight she couldn't shake; how part of her distress was that no matter what she thought of to make herself feel better, it felt pointless to her even before she began. She continued: "The truth is, I just don't know what's going on with me. By all accounts I should be happy." Between breaths she paused to look up at him.

His gentle smile in the face of her confession put her a bit more at ease so, in spite of being humiliated by her own words, she finished her thought, "Am I a hopeless case, or what?"

The good doctor studied her eyes for a few moments, took her hand in his, and spoke in light but serious tones. "Let me ask you a few simple questions and, depending upon your answers, I should be able to make an accurate diagnosis." And then in a slightly more serious tone he added, "But Katie, you must be totally honest with me. Will you?"

His question seemed to break some unseen dam in her and she felt a flood of apprehension. "What in the world is this about?" she thought to herself even as she managed to say, "Well, yes . . . of course I will."

"Good! Then let's get started shall we?" But he didn't wait for her reply and his first question took her completely by surprise. "Katie, do you have any regrets over things that happened to you in your past?"

Her hesitation wasn't from doubt over whether or not she had past regrets; of course she did. "And who doesn't!" her mind mocked the question. But through this mental clatter she was more curious than anything; after all, what on earth does such a question have to do with her degraded sense of well-being? A second later she nodded her head, indicating she did indeed have misgivings. "All right then," he continued, "That wasn't so bad was it? Let's keep going."

"Do you daydream a lot about better days to come?"

Surprised by the pressure behind her own words, she semi-snapped at what she felt was an invasion of her privacy. "What's wrong with that?" But he seemed to ignore this and went on to make a note in a small journal. "So then," he effortlessly brushed away the uncomfortable moment, "I guess that means you do. Good; let's keep going.

"Is it hard for you to be happy with yourself when you must be alone for a period of time that is not of your choosing?"

She looked down and momentarily lost herself in the weave of aged carpeting at her feet. Head still lowered, she agreed to the truth of this. He went ahead. "And what about anger or resentment? Are there people in your life—either living or passed on—who bring up unpleasant feelings in you when you think of them?"

Katie looked back up and noticed she felt as though she had to defend herself. "Well, wouldn't that be natural?" But he just made another note for himself and continued on, this time asking two questions at once: "Do you have any fear of being hurt by others; and would you say that you tend to be cynical and judgmental when it comes to considering the lofty aspirations of others—especially when they speak of looking for a love that won't betray their trust?"

Katie was becoming uneasy. The truth is she felt a twinge of pain just to hear these questions because she knew such things were true of her. The best she could do was to offer his inquiring eyes a kind of small grimace with her mouth, as if to say, "True enough."

The doctor must have felt her suffering because he told her, "Just a few more questions and we will be done. Are you someone who isn't happy unless you're busy all the time?"

Katie couldn't resist answering this question with one of her own, "Are you going to ask me any question about myself to which I can say, 'No, that's not true of me?'" The laugh they shared brought some welcome relief. Then he asked his last question:

"Do you ever catch yourself pushing away a certain indefinable sense of disappointment that you feel about people around you, especially those with whom you are the closest?"

She quietly lowered her head again as if to admit that this question, along with all the others that he had asked her, had to be answered in the affirmative. And while she didn't understand what these confessions had to do with her inability to find happiness, she did sense something was unfolding there in that little office. And so when she spoke again there was a bit of hope in her voice even though she masked it with a bit of sarcasm, "So, Doc, what's the prognosis? Is the patient hopeless, or what?"

Nothing in Katie's thirty-five years of existence prepared her for what she was to hear next. His answer struck home with the effect of a large mallet upon a metal gong, leaving her stunned, unable to formulate even a single thought.

The doctor took a small deep breath and spoke in a kind, but serious voice. "Katie," he said, "You have a broken heart."

A sudden sense of fear pushed itself out from the center of her, heading in two directions at once; but before it could spread the doctor stopped it cold, "No, Katie, physically there is nothing wrong with you." And just to relieve her obvious concern he chuckled quietly as he finished his thought, "So don't be afraid of some impending doom."

Taking him at his word, she began to search his eyes for some indication of what he meant by "a broken heart." And even though one part of her was now thinking that he must be joking, her intuition was on high alert. It was telling her that she had just been told some vital truth about herself. And even though she didn't understand this strange diagnosis, her life experience supported his finding. Unsure of how she really felt about what he had just told her, Katie looked to him for some kind of sign. Unexpectedly, the next thing she heard was the sound of her own voice asking, "What on earth do you mean . . . 'I have a broken heart'?"

"I'm sure you must be as surprised to hear this strange diagnosis as I was when, many years ago, I was told the same thing. But truth be known, Katie," he paused to ensure that he hadn't lost her attention, as he was about to tell her something equally staggering, "everyone on this planet, save a very few, has the same broken heart." Again he smiled to comfort her.

"But what do you mean by 'a broken heart,'" she implored him to expand on the idea. "How is it broken? What's wrong with it? Do you mean 'broken' like it needs healing or 'broken' as in doesn't work right, or what?" His answer caught her off guard.

"Is there any difference between the two?" Then he went on to say, "But if you're asking me if our suffering has its origin in something physical, then the answer is no. Our hearts are broken—meaning they don't work right—because they have been compromised." Katie was even more confused by his supposed clarification but she was intent upon getting to the bottom of his growing mystery.

"How is my heart *compromised*?" she asked. "What does that mean? Can't you be more specific?"

Again his answer caught her by surprise: "Well, to begin with, *Our heart is not created to be a self-filling instrument.*" She looked at him as if to say, "And what on earth is *that* supposed to mean?" He pulled up a chair and began to speak as he sat down next to her.

"Katie, think for a moment because in some ways you already understand what this means." Then he continued: "Don't we all have parts of us that are always telling us what we need to do—or what we have to get—in order to feel good about ourselves?"

She thought for a moment and nodded in agreement, so he went on, "Now comes the strange part. The day we win what we want, when we get the new relationship, the better job, or plan the trip of our dreams, we feel great, happy as a clam. But the *next day* or a little farther down the road something unforeseen comes and well, you know the drill, the next thing we know what we thought was the source of our contentment becomes the cause of our suffering!"

Again she nodded, thinking about the lost promise of a recent relationship that ended painfully when the man she thought was a prince turned into a toxic toad right in the midst of a silly disagreement. And yet, even as she was responding with her silent consent, she was struck by a contrary thought, and it was this that she gave voice to, "But what's wrong with wanting a nice relationship, or working to get nice things to call our own?"

"Not a thing, Katie, not a thing; all in all, these simple desires are not a problem in themselves. Our heart breaks as it does not so much because of *what* we want but because there are certain unconscious parts of our present nature that would have us believe that these things we want—or that we come to possess—have, in themselves, some power to fulfill us or to make us feel content." Then, to strengthen the point, he quieted his voice, "It is this unquestioned belief that lies at the root of our heartache because we find ourselves continually forming attachments to people and possessions."

"Even though I can see this is true, I still don't see the connection. What do attachments have to do with one walking around with a broken heart?"

"Everything Katie, only it's so obvious that no one sees it. Don't you see, we can't keep anything in this life. Our own lives don't even belong to us. It isn't a question of *if* things will change but a constant *when*. No part of life is static. All things are in a constant flux and only seem to hold still because there are parts of us that need to see them that way in order to feel secure. And so it goes. One's heart almost always feels as though one thing or another is trying to pull it apart. It finds itself living between two opposing forces. On one side there is that too-familiar sense of our self that feels as though we must hold onto what we have that makes us feel whole or otherwise face some terrible ordeal. And pulling away on the other side is the movement of reality itself: that undeniable river of life that comes along and washes away our happiness as it runs through its own inevitable changes beyond our ability to control."

Katie could feel a flood of new impressions pass through her as she allowed the doctor's comments to sink in. So much of what he said made sense to her in ways she felt she knew already, but what to do with these things she was hearing was beyond her at the moment, so she just sat there. Then one thought surfaced in her mind that seemed to tell her where everything she had just learned was heading: "So then," she paused to be certain that she had the right question, "If I understand what you have said then how do I begin to cure myself of this condition that, up until now, I had no idea was the cause of my unhappiness? I mean, what do I have to do to heal my own broken heart?"

The doctor smiled at Katie with genuine warmth. She *had* heard what he said; now he knew that it was only a matter of her making a few more discoveries and she would be well on her way to healing her own heart. But there was more she needed to know and even though he knew it would get a sharp reaction from her, he answered her question with what she took to be sarcasm. It wasn't.

He looked directly into her eyes and said, "We heal our heart by no longer injuring it."

Then, waiting for her anticipated negative reaction to pass, which it did, he smiled again and added, "The truth is that once we stop hurting ourselves, we realize we don't need ninety-nine percent of the things that we think we do to make us feel better about our life." Again she knew, intuitively, the truth of his words. And in spite of a frustration that was getting the better of her, she composed herself enough to ask her last question in another way:

"So where do I start, and with what? What must I do to free myself of this fight for the possession of my own heart?"

The doctor had the answer ready: "We must learn how to let go."

A surge of pressure pushed these words out of her; "That's *just* great!" she said. "But let go of what? How do we know what to hang onto and what to let fall away? There's got to be more to it than that! Besides, who knows what is the best . . ." He had started nodding halfway through her words and interrupted her thought midstream.

"Katie, that is exactly what I said the day I heard what I am now telling you. And of course you're right, to a degree. We must gain a higher understanding of the world around and within us if we wish to heal our hearts, and this wisdom requires new self-knowledge. So let me tell you the short story that my friend told me the day I learned about all this. I am sure it will help you to better understand how letting go is one and the same with the work of healing a broken heart.

REALIZE AND RELEASE THE ROOTS
OF PAINFUL ATTACHMENTS

Celeste was a happy young girl—happier than anyone else, she often thought to herself. After all, her every day was spent alongside her father taking care of the royal gardens. Hummingbirds and bright butterflies were her daily companions and there was always something growing in the garden that seemed to need only the attention that she could give it. And though her days always came to an end before she felt like they should, it wasn't as if her life was an idle one spent in childish dreams. She had real responsibilities.

Celeste and her father shared a simple life. Their modest cottage was tucked away in a corner of a small kingdom and their good fortune was not without a certain price. After all, her father had been given a highly coveted title by king's decree and everyone knew that such grants always came with higher accountability.

Officially he was Keeper of the Royal Roses, and, as best Celeste knew at her young age, her father had one primary job: to ensure that the royal couple never went a day without the joy of knowing that their loyal citizens were sharing the beauty of their royal gardens. But what she couldn't have known was that this part of her father's work was his least important task and that upon his shoulders lay a far greater responsibility, which is where our story begins.

One day while Celeste was busy by herself weeding around a new planting of tiny yellow roses in the west wing of the gardens, she heard her father call to her from a part of the compound generally considered off-limits to her. When she made it over to where she could see him waiting for her, she was taken by surprise.

He was standing in front of a pair of great wooden gates, behind which she had never been allowed. This was a walled-off area of the royal gardens, which she knew little about other than the fact that each week her father spent a great deal of his time working there on his own. It had long been obvious to her that something in there was considered a great secret, and the thought of learning what was hidden behind these doors made her heart race in anticipation. It took everything she had not to break into a run and even though she did manage to walk most of the way there, apparently it was not enough to conceal her excitement. For as soon as she was in range of his voice she heard her father say, "Yes, my sweet, that's right. The time has come." And with that he pulled open the large gates.

Moving her eyes past and beyond the swinging gates as fast as her vision could enter the compound, at first Celeste thought she had caught sight of sapphire waters from a secret lake that no one knew about. Commonsense ruled out this impression even as it formed in her; such a thing couldn't be true! Yet, what was this? Then she gasped and pulled her hands up over the top of her head as if to keep it from popping off.

She turned round to smile at her father and, gaining his silent permission, began to walk forward into what was a sea of heavenly blue roses, unlike anything she had ever seen in her life. Then something totally unexpected happened.

As she moved ahead and among the roses something about their scent pushed its way into her mind and seeded itself there. A moment later it felt like this delicate fragrance found its way into her eyes. She had to stop walking because it seemed for a moment like she couldn't see. But that wasn't it at all. In fact, a second later, she suddenly felt like she *could* see for the first time. It was unnerving.

As she stood there, she felt herself disappearing into the deep blueness before her, even though she was never more aware of her own distinctive nature. Unity and uniqueness became one thing, like the way a painting captures at once the whole of a scene even though the image itself is the work of a thousand separate brush strokes. Her mind struggled to make sense of its own enhanced perception; it couldn't, yet what she was experiencing was undeniable.

Each blue rose was alive and complete, radiating a composure and poise: a perfect tiny replica of some greater reality. Not one petal was out of place; in fact it was more like each one had been assigned both position and property from the beginning of time.

As the moment continued unfolding she realized that colors had fragrances of their own and that the delicate scent of each rose was a part of its color. She let go of trying to understand because she could also see that it only interfered with what she was learning. Even the sound of her father's voice calling to her was a precious part of the moment. It wasn't until he touched her on the shoulder that she realized her attention was being asked for. Reluctantly she came back, and when her eyes were her own again to command, she looked up to see him smiling at her as though he knew where she had been. He explained much to her in the sweet hour that followed.

"These," he said, gesturing with his arms before him and opening up both of his hands as if to catch a falling rain, "are the King's roses."

With this he took Celeste's hand in his own and, as he continued speaking, they walked together toward the heart of the garden. "There are none like them anywhere in the world. They are as rare as they are unknown, and those who are fortunate to receive one are granted a gift that this world doesn't yet know how to measure. This gift is a love that never dies."

Somehow Celeste knew exactly what he meant, as well as why he was speaking to her in these new and serious tones. She squeezed his hand to let him know what she couldn't find words for. They reached a small stone bench and sat down together.

"Today," he looked directly into her eyes, "if you wish it, you are going to be given one of the King's blue roses to keep as your own. That is," he went on to explain, "only if you agree to care for it like nothing else you have ever owned. Would you like that Celeste?"

Her wide-open eyes and ear-to-ear smile answered him in the affirmative. Seeing this, he reached down under the bench and pulled out a small earthen pot that held a single blue rosebud resting on a young, green stalk. Instinctively she reached out for it, but he did not give it to her.

"One step at a time, Celeste. Here is what you must do to take care of your new charge. First, you should find a special place known only to you and place the pot there, keeping in mind that your rose should receive plenty of sunlight and fresh air. And every day you must check it to see if it needs water. Be careful to pull out any small weeds that may have come to seed in its soil. But there is one thing that your blue rosebud needs more than anything if it is to grow strong and flourish," and he paused to make sure that she was paying careful attention, "You must love it every day. That is the one thing it cannot live without. Will you do these things as I have asked?"

"Oh yes, father, I promise. I *promise*." And with that he handed her the king's blue rose.

Everything went smoothly enough for the first month or so. Celeste did exactly as her father had commanded of her. In no time at all the little blue rosebud began to open; a second bud appeared even as the stalk that supported it grew in stature. And as its loveliness grew with each passing day, so did Celeste's wish to spend more and more time attending to it. But something changed in the sixth week; something went wrong. It wasn't that noticeable at first, but she was sure that the blue rose had begun to droop.

At first Celeste thought maybe it was because of too much water, so she cut back for a few days, but this did nothing to retard the now-alarming rate at which her rose was losing its luster. And so, even though she didn't want to tell her father about it for fear he might take her blue rose away, she went to him with her problem. His reaction was nothing like what she expected.

"Well," he said, "come on then. We had better go take a look at what's going on. Lead me to your rose!" he said in a teasing tone.

When they reached the place where Celeste had put her potted rose down on the ground her father walked around it a few times, bent down and lightly fingered a few petals, and in a matter-of-fact kind of voice told her, "You know, sometimes the King's blue roses don't like certain places for reasons known only to them; maybe too much light, maybe not enough; who knows? Hard to say for sure. At any rate," he said as he turned and started walking away, "best to find another place for it—I think that will do the trick."

Celeste couldn't understand why her father seemed so unconcerned; after all, wasn't he the one who had told her about the importance of these blue roses? But a moment later her mind gave her a glimpse of another place where her rose might be happier; in fact, she was sure of it. With this happy thought she reached down to pick up the small pot off the ground.

What happened next caught her off guard; it was so unexpected! The pot seemed stuck to the earth—like it was glued there! So, collecting her will, she gave it a small tug, thinking maybe some dirt had dried around the clay bottom; but instead of the pot coming free, she noticed that her action had caused a kind of shudder to pass through her blue rose.

Celeste didn't notice the fear that crept into her heart over this uncertain situation and neither was she conscious of the anger now telling her that no *stupid pot* was going to stop her from doing what she wanted to do with it. She grabbed hold of it with a new determination and gave a mighty yank! A second later she felt herself sink; for it wasn't the pot that came up off of the ground, but the blue rose had been roughly pulled down into its potting soil. She stared in disbelief at the damage. Some of its roots were now exposed, and the blue baby rose itself could barely stand upright. She was running to find her father before she even knew her feet were moving, her mind racing to find ways to explain why she wasn't at fault.

The odd thing was that after she had spilled out her heart about the unwanted accident he didn't seem that surprised. And try as she might, she couldn't tell what he was thinking as they walked together back toward the scene of Celeste's heartache. All she knew was that he didn't seem displeased with her, and this was a relief in itself. A moment later they were standing over the limp-looking rose.

As he knelt down on the ground alongside the now slightly leaning small pot, he indicated with both a smile and a tilt of his head that he wanted Celeste to do the same, which she did. Then, with his left hand supporting his weight, he took his right hand and gently pulled on one side of the pot, slightly exposing its bottom. "Look, Celeste," he told her, "Get down here with me and look under the pot. What do you see?"

She angled her head to where she could see the view he wanted her to, and she could barely believe her eyes. Reddish-black and brown roots had all but swallowed the bottom of the clay pot, pushing their way up from the earth beneath the pot and right into its drainage holes. She had never seen anything like this before. No wonder she couldn't lift the pot off the ground. These roots had it tied down to the earth! She looked back up at her father with a "Now what do we do?" bewildered expression, to which he replied, "No problem." And with that he drew from his work belt a small pair of sharp-looking scissors and began snipping away one by one at the invading roots.

Celeste watched closely as, snip by snip, the little clay pot began to be cut free. Then, about half way through the task her father handed her the scissors, handles first saying, "Now, you do it."

She was very tentative at first, but imitating his actions as closely as she could, she reached under the pot and continued cutting away the invading roots. While she continued cutting, her father explained what had happened to her blue rose.

"In this world of ours," he said, "there are naturally opposing forces that often appear to be set against what is good and whole, like when some sickness overtakes us, or when it doesn't rain when it should and everything suffers." He went on, being careful to choose his words, "These forces are a part of Nature herself. And yet, whatever form they may assume in life to express their individual nature, in the long run, these elements all work to serve the greater good.

"But Celeste," he continued as he watched her cutting through more of the twisted bands of dark roots, "there are other forces loose in this world that intend to stand in the way of beauty, wholeness, and happiness. Such creatures live to interfere with what is lovely and divine; they don't want what is good to succeed in flourishing on this earth. In a sense, these negative forces and their myriad forms belong to this world in much the same way as cave-dwelling bats belong to the dark nights they wing through." She stopped cutting for a moment to look up at him, wanting to understand the unspoken meaning behind his words.

He continued, "These roots that you are cutting away grew up from beneath your blue rose in order to steal into her developing roots. Fortunately you caught them before they could do any real damage. They belong to a certain order of life that can only live by thievery, and these creatures can only thrive as long as they remain undetected."

Nodding his own head as if confirming the point to himself, he finished the thought, "They are born in the dark, live in the dark, and desire the whole of our world to be as they would have it: a place of perpetual darkness." And as if reading Celeste's mind he added, "And these forces of falseness hate all blue roses."

"But I didn't see any evidence of these dark roots when I was with you in the King's garden," she protested.

"That's right," he said, "and you won't. Against a mature King's rose such things are powerless; but whenever the opportunity presents itself they will sneak into a young root system like this one to try and steal what the baby rose needs to develop and bloom. In truth, these dark roots are pathetic—powerless except for their cunning invisibility." And with that, Celeste cut through the last of the roots. The clay pot was free and so was her blue rose; but it didn't look very happy.

"It's alright," said her father, sensing her distress over the appearance of her rose. He stroked the back of her hair with his hand to comfort her. "All it needs now is a bit of extra love and it will recover without any problem. But you will be careful now wherever you set it down, won't you?"

But Celeste didn't answer. She was already on her way to a secret spot she knew of where, with her attentive care, her blue rosebud would grow up to live in a world beyond the reach of the dark roots of this world.

WHAT YOUR HIDDEN HEART REALLY WANTS

"And that's the end of that story, Katie," said the doctor. Then he looked directly at her and raised his eyebrows in an exaggerated manner, as if to ask whether she *got it*. She was shaking her head softly back and forth in disbelief and he took this as a good sign. He knew that some of what he had wished to impart had found its way home. But just to assure himself, he added a final comment.

"So you see, Katie, the True Nature of one's own heart is not broken at the outset. Far from it. She is the baby blue rose in our story: perfect, poised, full of the fragrance of life, innocent and potentially an invulnerable resident of the King's garden." He collected his thoughts and continued on with the idea:

"So when one's heart gets broken, it's really only because it has been pulled apart—caused much in the same way as Celeste's little blue rose nearly came apart when she tried to pull it loose from the ground. And like that baby rose was nearly a victim of the dark roots that had grown up into it, something similar happens to us. We talked about this earlier on when we spoke of that painful tug of war in one's heart—how a certain part of us wants what *it* wants, and how another reality, one that is greater than this desire, steps in to oppose it." Katie indicated she was following his line of thought so he leaned forward to strengthen their growing communication.

"This is the point: the more we believe, as we are inclined to do, that there exists something outside of us with the power to make us happy and whole, the more attached we become to these imposter ideas and those deceptive desires that weave into our hearts. These sensation-packed, but illusionary desires are the roots of this world that sneak into us. And the more we identify with these pleasing sensations, which are essentially on loan to us from the images in which they are stored, the more a painful dependency is born in us. Now it feels to us that without this person or object of our desire we will have to spend our lives without what we only have imagined has made us feel whole."

He paused for a moment as if to look into his own thoughts, and then, having found what he needed, went on. "Given this seemingly natural but false conclusion, what else can one do but live in fear of anything that threatens to change these conditions?" He took a deep breath, both to collect himself and to give Katie a chance to take in what he was telling her.

"Do you see what I'm saying, Katie? It's inevitable: fear strangles love; it kills compassion. Such fear suffocates the heart by telling it that it will lose its joy should it lose the object it derives its joy through. This message really only causes the heart to cling all the more tightly to its desire. And so willingly, yet unknowingly, the heart closes itself off from life—effectively blind to the fact of how this set of restrictions accomplishes exactly the opposite of what it really wants: freedom to love. And it goes that with each unconscious cycle like this, one's heart becomes that much more entangled in the very system of roots that are wrecking it. The more it is compromised like this, the more it gradually looses its simplicity; the native openness of one's heart is transformed into an unnatural suspiciousness. Then the only things it knows to look for in life are more of the very desires and attachments that betrayed and helped to shatter it in the first place!"

Katie took a deep breath, exhaled completely, and looked up at an old ceiling fan that was slowly circulating above her. As she watched it, she couldn't help thinking how round and round her life had gone so far, and how today was the day she knew things would change. It was in this spirit that she spoke:

"Tell me more about letting go, please. I really want to know."

"Letting go does not happen by accident, any more than a bird flies without first taking to the sky. Both acts are leaps of a kind, but as you will come to see, both are as natural to life as a dolphin is to the open sea."

With this he reached beneath the stack of papers next to his desk and pulled out a paperback book. And just by the way he handled it, Katie could tell this had to be an old friend of his. She was right. He handed the book to her.

Her voice was playful, as she had already begun to feel better, "And what have we here?"

"This little treasure is the book my friend gave to me on the day when I learned what I have just told you." He grinned openly.

"Now this book belongs to you, Katie. Take it with you. Keep it near. Study its lessons. Love what it tells you and, more importantly, learn to love what it shows you about your own entangled heart. Within its pages is everything you need to know about how to carefully, ruthlessly, cut away the roots of this world that have stolen into your heart. Embrace the insights it reveals and within you will develop a Living

Light that will not only heal your broken heart but will also keep it whole and happy forever."

Katie drew the book near to her and, without another word, left the good doctor's office to start her new life. She smiled the whole way home.

In your hands right now is the very same book Katie took with her that day. Welcome its knowledge, work with its principles, and watch how letting go and growing happier soon become one great healing action.

ASK THE MASTERS

QUESTION: I know it's not just me; everyone I know is so restless, moving around all the time! Why is it so hard for us to be quiet and at peace with ourselves?

ANSWER: *Thou hast formed us for Thyself, and our hearts are restless till they find rest in Thee.*

—Saint Augustine

QUESTION: What happened to us that our hearts are the way they are? What will it take for us to make real changes in our lives?

ANSWER: *Soon the child's clear eye is clouded over by ideas and opinions, pre-conceptions and abstractions. Simple free being becomes encrusted with the burdensome armor of the ego. Not until years later does an instinct come that a vital sense of mystery has been withdrawn. The sun glints through the pines, and the heart is pierced in a moment of reality and strange pain, like a memory of paradise. After that day. . . we become seekers.*

—Peter Matthiessen

KEY LESSONS IN REVIEW

1. The endless emotional sensations that enter into—and that temporarily possess the heart—are not the truth of the heart any more than the sun's baking heat, or a winter's freezing sleet, are the same as the sky they fill as they pass their way through it.

2. In the same way as a plot of standing ground cannot be transformed into a fertile, productive field without dedicated work to overturn its compacted soils, neither can our own souls be expected to reveal the riches of their native contents without us first awakening to what lies hidden within the darkened earth.

3. Our attachments are never to a certain thing or person but only to how the image of this person or object that we hold so closely in our minds allows us to experience ourselves. An attachment is not to a particular thing itself, but to the love we have of certain familiar sensations that our embracing of this image mechanically stimulates us to feel.

4. It is his wants and desires that disturb the waters that he longs in his heart to be still. This is the contradiction in consciousness that is reconciled only in God's will.

5. Whenever we put ourselves on the side of what we know is true, then the truth takes our side, lending us what is noble, needful, and divine. Truth sees to it that we are strengthened by wisdom, sheltered by light, and that our hearts know the peace of having fulfilled her plan.

CHAPTER TWO

Uncover the Secret
Treasure of Your True Self

Here is a timeless secret. It is as big and as powerful as is our willingness to discover the truth about our nature. *We each live—moment to moment—in a world the size of our understanding.* This means many encouraging things, beginning with this important discovery: When we feel small, of no consequence, or emotionally powerless to rise above some pressing pain, it's because we are living in and from unconscious parts of ourselves that are, in themselves, narrow and cut off from the bright and broad flow of Real Life. From this more psychological perspective, it is easy to see how in moments like these we might be deceived into believing that aching is the best we can do. Now let me give you a simple illustration of how it happens that we find ourselves captives of this constricting inner condition.

Some years ago you could buy special drinking straws that turned plain milk into chocolate milk. The insides of these straws were coated with a cocoa-like substance. When you drew the milk through the straw into your mouth, the milk would dissolve the chocolate coating and lend the milk its flavor. Well, in much the same way, whenever we look at ourselves or our lives through the eyes of these low-level states, we draw our sense of self through their restricted content. We take on the "flavor" of that negativity and everything seems cramped, dark, or futile. But here is the key lesson:

Even though there are times in our lives when it feels as if happiness has shut us out—or that conditions that seem to be beyond our ability to deal with are closing in on us—the truth of these moments is not as it appears. We have not reached the end of what is possible for us to become—we have only reached the end of our present understanding. Now here is a deeper look at this crucial insight: The only things that belittle us, that dominate us, or that cause us to despair over our lives are those unseen parts of us that dominate the way in which we see our life. Said in yet one more way, no one ever feels small in life who hasn't first been fooled into believing that there is nothing bigger than those small thoughts and feelings through which he or she is looking at life.

Imagine trying to gauge the majesty of a mountain through a microscope and you have a glimpse of what we face when realizing the unlimited estate of our Hidden Self. It isn't that we need to add bigger or brighter things to our lives to make us feel better about ourselves. We have all tried looking at life through rose-colored glasses and who can still believe that adding some new tint to the shade of one's troubles is the same as ridding oneself of their shadows?

What we really need is a whole new understanding of life—one that is realized through a new order of awareness that lets us see how we mistook ourselves for being small in the first place! A special short story will help us to open our eyes to a surprisingly higher self-possibility.

HIDDEN WITHIN YOU IS A GIFT TOO BIG TO SEE

In days now thought distant to us but perhaps not as far as one would imagine, the queen of a great country sent one of her ladies-in-waiting to find her daughter, Princess Constance, and to tell her that her mother wished to see her right away.

At the time that she was summoned, Constance was thoroughly engrossed, serving an elegant make-believe tea party to equally imagined royal visitors, so you can understand her disappointment at having to excuse herself from her guests! But she was a good daughter and her mother, the queen, had taught her from early on that part of the noble life often meant having to sacrifice one's own desires for the sake of a greater order. So off she went, running with her long hair ribbons trailing behind her like thin streaks of a white wind-swept cloud.

When she came to the great wooden door of her mother's bedroom chamber she stopped, caught her breath, collected her composure, and knocked their special secret knock that told her mother, "It is I, Constance, come to see you." And as usual, without waiting, she pushed open the doors and rushed inside.

Before she had even made it halfway across the smooth stone floor, she heard her mother say, somewhat sternly, "Constance, come here and sit down next to me."

As she finished her walk over to where her mother was seated, her eyes searched her mother's for some sign of just how much trouble she was in. But when she reached the small tufted bench it was not a reprimanding look but a smile that welcomed her. And so, sliding her hands into her mother's open hand, she sat down next to her. Instinctively Constance knew she should be quiet, and for a moment the two of them shared an unspoken affection.

Constance had long since come to recognize the difference between the voice of *mom* and that of her mother, the ruling monarch. Now, it was the voice of the monarch that spoke. "Constance," the queen began slowly, "even though you are still but a child, you are now old enough to receive the gift I have been holding for you since the day you were born."

She looked down at Constance to ensure her daughter was paying attention, but she didn't have to worry about that. Constance met her glance with a big open grin that fairly shouted, "Tell me more!" In fact, the clamoring of her own thoughts had grown so loud that Constance barely heard another thing her mother told her that afternoon. Out of all that was said, all she remembered as she left the royal chambers some time later was one thing: whatever the nature of this royal gift that her mother had for her, she would receive it some time after breakfast the next morning. But who could wait that long?

Constance ran all the way back to her quarters in the west wing of the castle where, from almost halfway across the room, she threw herself onto her bed. Her mind didn't stop racing the entire afternoon. And what a contest it was; one after another some spectacular vision of what might be hers would run through her mind's eye—only to be replaced, as if by magic, by an imagined something even more grand. The possibilities were endless; after all, being the daughter of a great queen who ruled over a vast country, she was heir-elect to all its wealth.

What if she was about to be given her very own golden coach with white stallions and four royal footmen all dressed in black? Of course that would do; but better yet would be a small castle, nothing too large, just big enough to entertain her friends in a palace of her own, some place where adults couldn't interfere with her private affairs. Maybe she was to receive her royal dowry! Her heart leaped as she thought of that day she first sneaked into the royal treasury room. In it were countless open chests overflowing with jewels and pearls of all shapes and sizes, bolts of rare silks, and more gold and silver coins than could be counted in a lifetime. And so Constance spent the rest of her day and all that evening in dreams fit for a princess. But these same dreams wouldn't let her sleep, and she spent what was one of the longest nights of her short life.

The next morning, after a compulsory breakfast that she could barely eat, Constance looked up and saw her mother standing in the open archway of the great hall where she took her meals. With one wave of her white-gloved hand, the queen beckoned Constance to follow her and disappeared down the long passageway. Constance was quick to follow; and when she caught up to her mother she was surprised to find her standing in the courtyard, about to board the royal coach. Where were they going? And why did it have to be *now*? This was not the way things should be going. But, swallowing her disappointment at this delay in receiving the gift she had been prom-ised, she quietly stepped inside the coach. No sooner had she taken her appointed seat on the padded bench across from her mother then, with a sudden start, they were off.

The next four hours were the worst Constance had ever experi-enced, that is, until they pulled up in front of the royal lake cottage where she was told they would be spending the night. Her mind was wracked with questions: Could her mother have forgotten her gift? Was she being put through some kind of test to determine her wor-thiness? Should she speak up or just continue on with her act and pretend that whatever mother wants is her wish as well? Rather than let others know that her own thoughts were consuming her, Constance chose to stifle her desires and concerns.

That evening passed as slowly as did the royal parades she so hated to sit through. The only thing that made it tolerable was her hope that tomorrow would be her day. No such luck! Early that next morning, while snooping around inside the royal coach for the gift she hoped her mother might have brought along, Constance received stunning news from one of the drivers. The plan for the day called for an eight-hour ride north to the royal mountain chalet. She almost cried out loud, "This can't be!" but caught herself in time. After a quick bite to eat, and not one word about anything important, like the whereabouts of her royal gift, off they went again.

Even though the countryside was brilliantly decked in pre-autumnal colors, the ride along the tree-lined road seemed to go on forever. Finally, just at dusk, they pulled up to the royal Castle of the North to find a banquet prepared and waiting for them. Constance thought maybe this party was the front-runner of better things to come, but the evening passed without a single mention of her gift. And, in spite of the soothing sounds of the great river rising up from the foot of the mountain below, she barely slept a wink. "Tomorrow I will end this," she kept telling herself. But she couldn't put an end to the stream of her own tormenting thoughts. She felt helpless. And, as she would soon come to discover, things were not going to get better.

For another five days Constance, her mother, and their small entourage of attendants pressed ahead—one night at the royal vine-yards, the next day touring the royal mines. Then a day's ride through open plains and valley fields, they inspected the granaries and then went on to their coastal estate for a sunset cruise aboard the flag-ship of the Royal Navy. What could she do? As it seemed to be her only option, Constance decided to play the waiting game. Better for her, she thought, not to appear as though all she wanted was her mother's gift, even though she could think of nothing else. But as the saying goes, "The best laid plans of mice and men oft go astray. . . ."

It was late into the seventh day of their journey when Constance realized that, on the far side of the great lake around which they were traveling, she could see the outline of the royal cottages where they had spent their first night. She shuddered as she quickly calculated this position in her mind. It could mean only one thing, and it wasn't good: they were riding on the lakeshore's east road that would take them deep into the southern region of her mother's kingdom. And this meant at least another week of traveling with the silent torment of not getting her gift. What had been her controlled calm could no longer hide the storm beneath it. She cried out.

"Mother, why do you withhold my gift, the special one you had promised me eight long days ago? What have I done to deserve the punishment of this long journey without you even mentioning a word of it?" In that instant the short distance between her and her mother suddenly felt as empty as she did for having poured out her heart in this way. She looked back into her mother's eyes intending to be strong, but instead caved into the sadness that she could see in them.

"Mother," she spoke under her breath, barely audible for the sound of the coach wheels rolling along on the graveled path. "I am sorry for my shameful remarks. Please forgive me. You have my promise this will never be mentioned again."

But instead of answering her, the queen leaned forward and bid the drivers to stop the carriage. Then, after allowing a moment to pass for the road dust to settle, she reached over and flung open the coach door. "Come with me," she instructed her daughter. Somewhat reluctantly Constance did as she was told and followed close behind her. They walked slowly down to the edge of the lake.

She felt the mounting pressure of her own raging emotions as they stood together in the setting sun, but more than anything else it was the terrific silence between them that made her start apologizing all over again for her *un-royal* behavior. But before she could get through even the first few words of the regret that she was feeling, her mother cut her off.

"Never mind all that, my sweet, it's all right; really it is," she said in a comforting voice. "Let's not have one more word about this. Besides," she continued, "I must assume some responsibility for what has happened."

She reached out and placed one arm around her daughter's shoulder and, gently pulling her nearer to her, began to turn slowly with her in a three-hundred-and-sixty-degree circle. "So now," she went on speaking, "let me give you my gift in a way that cannot be mistaken."

And with this the queen extended her other arm in a broad sweeping gesture that took in the whole country before them and quietly spoke these words: "Listen to me, daughter of my heart. For the last seven days and nights we have been riding through your gift, only you couldn't realize what had been given to you because it was too big for you to see!"

She looked up at her mother to ensure that her ears had not deceived her, and when her eyes met a royal smile beaming back at her confirming the immensity of the moment, she knew it was true. So Constance smiled back at her not only in gratitude for this immeasurable gift, but also for the experience of a strange new feeling now coursing its way through her. For the first time in her tender young life, humility touched her heart. And in these brief seconds of this stirring in her something else was equally evident: she could not separate this powerful new sensation from the revelation that had given it birth. *How small had been her own imagination—desiring only such trivial things had kept her from seeing what was right before her eyes the whole time.*

As she gave her mind over to explore this discovery, another revelation struck home with equal power: all the suffering she had endured over the last week had been for nothing. She looked back up at her mother to say something more, but her mother spoke first. And from her words it was obvious that her mother already understood everything that Constance had just now realized. "Yes, daughter; that is correct. Everything you see around you not only belongs to you now but also has always been yours from the moment that you were born."

A NEW KIND OF SEEING THAT HELPS SET YOU FREE

We all know what it is like to be held captive of the little things in life—those petty concerns and small desires that steal their way into how we look at our lives and pit us against anyone or anything seen as trying to take away our anticipated desire. Here is a short list of these little troublemakers that often make big trouble for us whenever we mistake them for being our friends:

1. Unrealistic expectations that others should treat us only as we imagine they should

2. Strong attachments to even the smallest and strangest of our possessions

3. Pressing convictions that no one else sees things as clearly as we do

4. Nagging resentments from relationships past and present

5. Perfect certainty that no one is permitted to interrupt our pleasures

How can we say for sure that these conditions are little more than *big nothings* in the scheme of things? We have all been through those tell-tale moments in our lives when, due to a crisis of some kind beyond our control, we are momentarily able to see where we had lost sight of what was really worthwhile.

Perhaps we are the kind of person who is always complaining about some small ache or pain, and then we suddenly learn that someone we love faces a life-or-death challenge. Maybe we think that we are the only one on earth who suffers emotionally in the way that we do, and then comes that moment when, in lashing out at someone for being so uncaring about our situation, we not only see that he or she is suffering as well, but also that we are the cause of it. Or maybe we're lucky enough to be with someone who has less in life than we do, but who is willing and happy to share what little he or she has in spite of what tomorrow might bring. In such moments, if we still have a human heart, we realize in humility that we have been blind to the existence of our own greater estate.

In moments like these which, truth be told, are too far apart for our own spiritual good, we make this shocking but wonderful discovery: we have been lost in some little part of ourselves, unconscious of the influence of our own self-centered desires, as well as of the cost this unsuspected selfishness exacts on everyone around us.

Even more important than this initial revelation is the following one that appears within our new awareness. We can now see, by the faintest light, that *we had mistaken ourselves for someone we are not*! And in this same self-awakening we are granted that first priceless glimmer of self-knowledge that is sought after by all who would uncover the truth of themselves: we are beginning to see that we have been playing host to an unconscious nature that is not only blind to the world that it binds us to, but also that would have us believe that its little selfdom is the same as the actual great estate of our True Nature.

How can such a deception take place in us and go undetected? We would never willingly agree to be the blind agent of that which makes another human being ache, let alone hurt our own chances to grow into a kind and compassionate being. And yet the evidence reveals that we are indeed living under the sway of self-compromising influences that are invisible to us. The following short story not only reveals the secret nature of this strange servitude, but also provides real solutions to help us start letting go of that which wants to hold us down.

Paul had grown tired of living in the rush and rage of the big city where he was born and longed for a quieter life. Within him stirred the echoes of days past when he once thought he might like to live closer to nature. And one day, as it often happens for those who break away from that which never made them happy, events transpired that caused Paul to give notice to company and friends alike. After saying his goodbyes and making a few other necessary arrangements, he made his move upstate to a rural setting about a half-hour outside a small country township.

It was late in the afternoon when he pulled up to the entrance of the modest ranch house that he had leased with the option to buy. It sat in the middle of twenty acres of pastured woodlands, and Paul noticed two things right away when he stepped out of his car. First, he felt safe, and he mentally remarked to himself that this was a feeling he could definitely get used to! He took a deep breath and relished the air. Except for a small flock of happy birds that were singing from somewhere out in the neighboring field, all around him the world was hushed.

At the same time Paul noticed he was starting to feel exhausted just thinking about all the work it would take to get his new place in shape. "Oh well," he thought to himself; "first thing tomorrow I'll go to town and get supplies." With that settled in his mind he carried his belongings into the house and later on, lying in bed that night with the bedroom windows wide open, he fell asleep in the midst of planning his new life.

The next morning when Paul drove into town he was surprised to find such a large, well-stocked general store right in the middle of what he thought was no-where. But there was no disputing it; in this store there were dozens of divided rows filled with everything a person could need, from soup to the metallic nuts he would need to repair a broken cabinet door. The only thing there didn't seem to be any of was someone to help him shop!

"Now what?" he thought as looked down at his three-page list and then over to the one counter in the store. Behind the counter sat an elderly man who seemed to be taking an afternoon nap at ten in the morning. How on earth was he going to get everything done in the time he had set for this shopping trip if there was no one to show him where to look for what he needed? But Paul pushed back this wave of frustration and walked over to ask, as politely as he could given the uncooperative conditions he had found himself in, where he might find dish soap and other kitchen supplies. The kindly man behind the counter told him where to look, and with a compulsory nod of thanks, Paul was on his way.

Scarcely three minutes later, kitchen supplies safely aboard his shopping cart, Paul couldn't find the special canned tomatoes he liked to use for his pasta sauce. He saw beans, creamed corn, and more kinds of chili than he knew ever existed, but no crushed Italian tomatoes. The next moment a heat born of impatience flared up and he took off his coat. He let this pass as best he could and walked a foot or two down the aisle in the direction of the checkout counter, where he half-shouted, "How about a little help over here?" A minute later the older gentleman appeared and politely pointed, just a few shelves down, to the goods Paul wanted.

For the next forty minutes this scene repeated itself about a dozen times. Each time Paul had to go out of his way to ask for directions to find what he wanted and he became increasingly agitated. As the voices in his head grew louder, his temper grew shorter. Finally, still unable to locate the last item on his list, and at the end of his ability to hide his anger over what he was sure was the most ineptly run store in the world, he let loose this irritation on the store keeper.

"It's impossible to find anything in this store," he complained bitterly. "There seems no rhyme or reason to where things are, and that's *if* someone could find the right shelf." His final assertion was intended to get a rise from the slightly bemused-looking storekeeper who was just standing there, quietly watching him go ballistic. "And I strongly doubt that I will ever come back to shop here again!"

Nothing was said between them for far too long, which made Paul start to feel foolish for his outburst but compared to what he was about to go through, this mild embarrassment would prove to be nothing. When the old gentleman finally spoke up it was in measured tones, "Well, sir, of course it's a free country, and you can do whatever you like; but as to it being hard to find items in this store, would you mind if I just pointed out one small thing you may have overlooked?" He took Paul's silent stare as consent to finish his thought:

"Well, anyway, should you decide to change your mind and come back, I will always be happy to help you in any way I can. But just in case you haven't noticed this yet, in this store," and he raised a finger and pointed above his head, "to find whatever you want, all you have to do is look up."

In what felt to him like an involuntary act on his part, Paul's eyes slowly followed the line of the man's raised hand to see what he was pointing to. A heartbeat later he almost fell over backwards. For there, just above him, lined up in perfect array over every single aisle, were dozens of carefully lettered, hanging signs. Paul blinked his eyes several times, like he couldn't believe what was in them. Each sign clearly indicated what could be found where, right down to individual brand names and their aisle number.

In that moment Paul felt a sort of shame come over him similar to a time he had all but forgotten when, years earlier in grade school, he had wrongly accused his best friend of stealing his lunch. But what had really happened was that Paul had been so nervous about his little league team's tryout that afternoon that he had left his lunch bag at home on the kitchen counter.

"Please, forgive me," he managed to get out of his mouth as he found himself living in two places at once and struggling to return to the present moment. "I don't know what came over me. I guess I was in such a hurry to get my hands on what I thought I had to have," and he smiled as best he knew how, finishing his apology, "that I was blind to what I needed to see."

"Sure, no problem," said the old shopkeeper, smiling back at Paul. "We've all been there; main thing is that everything is all right now, right?"

"Right," Paul said. And then, sensing it would be appropriate for the moment, he quietly added one last thought, "Thanks for the lesson." With this the old man nodded in silent understanding and returned to his place behind the counter where he would wait for the next customer.

There is a tried and true spiritual idea that few remember in these pressing times when everyone is in a rush to claim their place in the sun. Its simple message speaks volumes, and its wisdom applies to all of us, wherever we may be in our work to let go and live in the Now. And, as it relates to our story where Paul discovered just how blind one can be given the *right* circumstances, again the old saying goes: He couldn't see the forest for the trees!

Just as the small princess in our earlier story could not see the size of her mother's gift because the only thing that her young mind knew how to look for were littler things, so too Paul was temporarily blinded to the reality of his own inner condition: he could not see the sign boards above his head because the only thing his eyes could see was what his mind saw as being the problem. The lesson here is that just as the princess and Paul were unable to look beyond the *little things* occupying their minds, so too it rarely occurs to us to *look up* in order to receive the greatest gift in the world: the grand guidance that leads us to the realization that within us dwells a divine nature whose kingdom is our very own.

William Blake once wrote, "The roaring of lions, the howling of wolves, the raging of the storming sea, and the destructive sword are portions of eternity too great for the eye of man." And who hasn't felt at times as though we have settled outside the immensity of Real Life? Where so consumed are we with mundane concerns that what is grand and majestic about life might as well be taking place on a distant planet for all our ability to see it.

Yet, in spite of this glass through which we see darkly, somehow we do manage to recognize the truth of this spiritual blindness so that in this still-dim vision of ours there dwells, as the enlightened essayist Ralph Waldo Emerson writes, the seed of a great hope "we do not yet possess ourselves, and we know at the same time that we are much more."

One thing should be clear: not one of us would choose to live from a *Self* that determines what is possible for us to become in life by looking back upon who we have been. As long as this level of Self sits in charge of our consciousness, we remain cut off from the wellspring of wisdom that awaits us within. But now we have taken the first steps in securing the powers we must regain to reclaim our rightful place in Real Life. First comes the new self-knowledge with which we must work; then, from this, like the summer rose liberated from its spring bud, comes the strength of conviction we will need to proceed along the path and to succeed with our own awakening.

We have learned that our True Nature is not some static line drawn upon a horizontal plane, where access to what we may become depends upon what is already known. The truth is far from this. We are at our core a creature of the stars: beings whose original and celestial stuff is not only born of light, but also intended to live unbound.

It is this higher, yet still Hidden Self of ours that beckons us to realize and enter into a greater life. And though its whispered wisdom often gets lost in the din of all the other voices that tell us what we need and where to look for it, if we listen closely enough we can hear what our True Self would have us know: *Whenever we start to feel small it's only because we have unconsciously identified ourselves with life's little things.* Learning to let go and to live in the Now is the same as catching ourselves holding onto what limits us and then deliberately dropping these self-imposed restrictions.

ASK THE MASTERS

QUESTION: Whenever I read or spend time pondering truthful things I often feel as though nothing in the world can bring me down. In those moments I am the conqueror of all that had overcome me only minutes before. Can you shed some light on what helps lift me like this?

ANSWER: *In the presence of greater meaning all lesser meanings—that fill our ordinary mind full to the brim—shrink to their true proportions and cease to steal from us. For in the presence of greater meaning we are redeemed from everything small and trivial and absurd.*

—Maurice Nicoll

QUESTION: Why does it always feel as though life is pulling on me from two directions at once? On one hand I know I want a new and higher life, free from my past; but more often than not it seems as though I'm caught in a strange undercurrent that won't let me let go! I could really use some encouragement.

ANSWER: *"The great Architect of the universe conceived and produced a being endowed with both natures, the visible and the invisible: God created the human being, bringing its body forth from the pre-existing matter which he animated with his own Spirit . . . Thus in some way a new universe was born, small and great at one and the same time. God set this 'hybrid' worshipper on earth to contemplate the visible world, and to be initiated into the invisible; to reign over earth's creatures, and to obey orders from on high. He created a being at once earthly and heavenly, insecure and immortal, visible and invisible, halfway between greatness and nothingness, flesh and spirit at the same time . . . an animal en route to another native land, and, most mysterious of all, made to resemble God by simple submission to the divine will.*

—Gregory Nazianzen

KEY LESSONS IN REVIEW

1. We must stop searching for some kind of happiness *to come* and learn what it means for us to be whole in the present moment—for all forms of momentary happiness have proven themselves as little more than brightly colored clouds briefly set afire by the setting sun. The more we choose in favor of being awake to our own True Self, the sooner we will come to realize the timeless happiness that already awaits anyone who will seek it first.

2. Just as the echo of a voice that has shouted out, "Stop making all that noise!" is itself powerless to stop the one shouting, or to otherwise effect a change in its own harsh tone, so too is the level of Self that negatively reacts to any unwanted condition powerless to change its unpleasant experience of that moment it protests.

3. It is never the unwanted condition itself that has us stuck; it is that we are unknowingly hung up in habitual thoughts and feelings about our situation. To be new and live in the Now we must learn to see our lives from the part of us that *knows* our True Nature is not created to be a captive of anything!

4. Each life lesson gained, each timeless truth gleaned by going through what we would have rather not gone through, confirms a great secret unknown by the masses: the whole universe had to

have participated in that moment of our transformation, otherwise none of the necessary elements could have been in the right place at the right time to deliver that perfectly tailored lesson. Here, we find personal evidence of what new physics now professes as true. Our life sits at the very center of a universe that revolves around it. But to this wondrous discovery we must add one more insight: as this is true for my life, it is equally so for everyone else. *Each of us lives in the heart of this Great Center around which everything eternally turns.* The sooner we awaken to this great lesson—that all of us are at cause for the creation of our lives—the sooner will also pass away all of the conflict in this weary world of ours.

5. If we must dream, let us long for that life beyond ourselves, for who desires things already known, or otherwise imagined, in forms reconfigured from fantasies too well worn? Behold! It is the unknown life that calls to us from a desire untold—too distant and dark to be seen, but nearer to us than the very light in which we dwell.

CHAPTER THREE

Spiritual Secrets With the Power to Help Set You Free

When, centuries ago, William Shakespeare wrote the now famous words of Hamlet, "To be, or not to be, that is the question," his words touched upon something deep in the human psyche. The proof of their stirring sentiment should be self-evident, for this same self-inquiry causes those of us who hear these words today to also pause and ponder our own being. Perhaps the true staying power in this question, "To be, or not to be," is found not so much in what it says to us in words, but rather in its hidden spiritual implications. What this passage doesn't state, but nevertheless implies loud and clear is that to be, or not to be, is *not* our choice. We are conscious creatures—whether we choose to be or not!

In other words, to be or not to be conscious is not up to us; consciousness comes with being an organic creature on this planet. At lower levels we can see how all creatures—from sea bass to bugs—express their level of consciousness. Even flowers have some level of consciousness as evidenced by their phototropic activities. This level of simple consciousness implies awareness of the environment and the capacity to respond to it; but the consciousness of we human beings is of another order all together, one that runs far deeper than most people ever dare to explore.

You see, the question for us is not whether we will or won't have simple conscious awareness of the world around us. This level of our awareness is a given. The real question before those of us who would realize unconditional freedom is this: in which of the many worlds of consciousness that dwell within us do we wish to live?

If this last idea is new to you, a moment's consideration of what it implies will prove itself well worth your time, for here is an inescapable fact of life: I *am* whether or not what I am in that moment is who or what I want to be. We might as well try and hold a large beach ball under the waves of the ocean as to try and push away our own awareness of being, whatever that may hold for us. The good news is that we no longer need to live with any compromising state of Self once we have realized certain truths about ourselves, such as those about to be revealed.

Unlike lesser-level creatures that are not conscious of their own nature—and that cannot choose any other world of experience apart from the one they are drawn to by their own lower nature—we, as human beings, are unique in creation. We are created to be *self-conscious*.

In spiritual terms this means we may have an awareness of any of the infinite number of qualities that form the character of our own heart, mind, and soul; but that's not all. Within this same special feature of ours is hidden a greater gift. Not only may we enter into and know the undiscovered country that is the content of our own consciousness, but we can also learn to choose at what level of our own being we will live. It's true; unlike any other creatures, we alone may decide and then reside within that reality of ourselves to which we are drawn. If this idea surprises you, welcome to the wonderful world of higher self-knowledge! Let's learn more about our unique gift.

This level of higher conscious awareness empowers us to be one with all that exists in the kingdom of creation, much as one's own mind is created to know the content of its own thoughts. There is evidence to support this assertion.

We have all known that special sense of oneness that comes when we sit silenced by an inspiring sight. The sun sets and the clouds blaze, leaving our heart to feel as its own the multi-colored fire that paints the darkening sky. Who hasn't stood outside on a moonless night and been transported into a state of timelessness with the stars whose ancient light fills our upturned eyes? Even so, as soul stirring as such glimpses are, they remain as gold dust to the mother lode as we enlarge the depth of our self-study.

A HIGHER LESSON IN LIFE LEVELS
THAT LEADS TO A NEW LIFE

When Christ told his disciples that "My Father's kingdom has many mansions," he was doing more than just teaching them esoteric principles concerning their own unexplored being. For those who had ears to hear his words were, and still are, an invitation interpreted here: "Choose for yourself that mansion of mind or heart in which you would dwell. Where in the greater kingdom of consciousness would you like to live?" Again, our own experience confirms the possibility of this amazing spiritual potential.

We have all wandered through the many *mansions* that make up the world of our own thoughts and feelings. These are those psychological places within us that we move in and out of countless times each day. To illustrate just one example, there is that shelter of pride-filled thoughts we have about our Self and about how others should treat us. In its west wing are the fiery feelings that race through us when even casual acquaintances fail to fulfill our expectations. And, to enlarge the metaphor, in these very same dwellings that are made up of our demands, living on the floor just beneath them we find their neighbors. These are the negative emotions that not only blind us to the consequence of our own heated reactions, but whose room-mates quickly step into the fray, telling us to blame others for the troubles that always follow when we cling to our own mistaken assumptions!

As long as we live within the darkened mansion of these lower-level thoughts and feelings, unconsciously deriving our sense of self from identification with the stuff of our little lives, we must remain captives of their imperfect perspective. But there are other places in our hearts and minds, higher realms in this same interior kingdom, where we are free to live without such self-compromising limitations.

For instance, we can live in the *castle of noble ideas* about our own higher consciousness. Such enlightening concepts, along with the higher emotions they impart, shed helpful light on the nature of those self-defeating thoughts that trick us into entering their dark domain. These same liberating insights are the front-runner of new and expansive energies that pour into us whenever we are living in some littler world of ourselves and then step out of it into the wide-open spaces of our True Nature—a step that brings us to our next lesson in letting go and living in the Now.

As we look into the invisible realm of thoughts and feelings within us, we see a world of many different levels within levels, like one house with three different floors where each level in that house tells its own story. In this instance we might think of the upstairs rooms in a house, with windows that let in lots of light, as being similar to bright, uplifting thoughts; while negative states are the basement floor; a place void of light except for the red glow of a hot furnace. Using this simple analogy we can see that each level of the house we are living in reflects and projects the kind of environment found there.

When we speak in this way of there being "worlds within worlds," we are talking about something called scale. The whole idea that worlds are in scale to one another is an important concept for us to grasp, so you'll be glad to hear that you already know more about this special principle than you think! As a quick example, imagine how one inch appears on the thirty-six-inch scale of a yardstick. That one inch represents a fraction of the yardstick that contains it, so it is one thirty-sixth in the scale of a yard.

Another kind of scale we can study is how the structure and the movement of the atoms in a molecule is a tiny replica of our own solar system, complete with all of its orbiting bodies. Yet these two very different expressions of one underlying reality—a solar system whose primordial building blocks are a miniaturized microscopic version of itself—themselves share in a greater order of scale; one we need to understand in order to uncover the true nature of our Original Self.

Compared to the short lifetime of the orbiting bodies that make up any one molecule of matter, the planets in our solar system are virtually timeless. Again, in scale, these same heavenly bodies that fly through space have a relatively limited existence when weighed against the immeasurable void through which they orbit. It's with this last idea that we reach our most important insight concerning scale: as the lesser is always found within the greater, so this principle holds true with regards to time and the eternal. All that is created in time—all material worlds seen or not, including the kingdom of thoughts and feelings—dwell within what is the timeless Now. This eternal present is the invisible backdrop of all that is temporary, a principle and a promise that we study in depth in the next chapter.

Happiness, love, peace, compassion, and contentment are time-less states of being in the Now. In their original principle they are without form, having no beginning or end. These forces of the Living Light exist in themselves and have no cause apart from their celestial source, much as the sun exists apart from the life-giving light that radiates from the surface of its hydrogen heart. But for the time being, we relate to these states of higher consciousness through largely conditioned ideas about them. We search through popular ideas and socially accepted icons for the lasting fulfillment these celestial forces alone have the power to provide, a relationship that has as much in common with what is timeless as does a watch! And so we mistake the passing sensations of life as being the same as Real Life. That's where we get tricked. For not only are the depth and breadth of these self-generated sensations confined to the limited world of manufactured ideas from which they originate, but also in our identification with them, we have unknowingly agreed to live out our lives in their little world!

Awakening to who we are created to be is the first step in letting go of all that holds us captive. I have seen wild turkeys throw themselves up against a five-foot high wrought-iron fence trying to get out of the same yard they flew into only moments before. In moments of panic—such as when my wife would chase them out of her flower beds—these creatures forget that they have wings! We, too, have forgotten something: we are created to be unconditionally free. As a result of our spiritual forgetfulness we continue to throw ourselves against life, trying in vain to find for ourselves what can only be found through the conscious remembrance of our True Nature.

FREE YOURSELF FROM THE CAPTIVITY OF THE FALSE SELF

In some ways the work of letting go and living from our True Nature is simple. If we want to know the course of an uncharted river, or map a region of an unknown forest, we must enter into and explore that new world. We would think it silly for two people to argue about the nature of a remote valley—what life forms it holds, sustains, or denies—if these two people live near its entrance but never dared to explore it! Yet this is much of the way things are today when it comes to the hidden heart of higher spiritual consciousness. Christians argue with Buddhists; Hindus mistrust Muslims; Muslims fight with Jews. Wars are fought over who owns the rights to holiness! On and on goes the disagreement, getting nowhere and dragging everyone down with it. Does God have one face, many faces, or no face? Say to me the right words with the right inflection and we are "brothers." Answer incorrectly and, well, we all know what will happen. People despise and even try to destroy one another in the name of the God that they profess is love. It ought not be like this. It *need* not remain this way.

We are created and each of us is intended to discover the truth of ourselves within ourselves; no authorities are needed. Our lives—and all of our relationships as revealed in the present moment—are the ground we must plow. These soils, rendered receptive through conscious humiliation, are seeded with our intention to be kind and true to one another, to give up our selfish ways, and to willingly embrace whatever life lessons we need to further our inner development. These actions constitute the path of self-realization; its many footstones are the experiences we outgrow and let go of along the way. The concerns our conditioned lives place before these discoveries obscure the possibility of recovering our individual relationship with the Living Light. What does it take for us to begin softening this *ground* of ourselves so that the truth within us may flower?

We must learn to be with ourselves. We need to see the futility of trying to be anything other than awake to the moments of our life as they unfold in the Now. The insight that follows will strengthen our understanding of this timeless maxim, as well as our willingness to enact it.

The present moment and our awareness of it are one consciousness, much in the same way as a mirror and the object it reflects share the eye of the beholder. Let this idea soak in for a moment. Add to this insight the idea that we are always living in the Now—through which all our times pass without changing its eternal character—and we come to a truly astounding revelation. Everything there is for us to know about ourselves *is knowable Now.* The seemingly hidden purpose of our own existence awaits us Now . . . right within the stillness of our own awareness that is the witnessing background for life's passages.

But before we can experience the truth of this higher state of consciousness, before we can stand on the ground of ourselves that is the secret stuff of Reality, we are asked to quietly be who and what we are in the Now. To *do* this we must learn to let go of those parts of our present nature that are never quite pleased with what *is.* After all, doesn't it seem that we are always in some sort of a struggle to change whatever or whoever it may be before us that misses the mark? Which brings us to a special exercise designed to help us let go of the many false feelings of "I" that come over us when we start to feel negative toward some unwanted event. What exactly is a "false sense of I"? First, we will examine the nature of this self-created character from a broader perspective, and then we'll take a closer look at what must be done to drop it.

Imagine that we feel an angry flash pass through us for any of a hundred reasons. As this conflict-born heat makes its way through our psychic system, there is a natural registration of this disturbance within us. But at this early stage, in that surge of a heated sensation, there is just the mind's faint but growing awareness of a turbulent state. Milliseconds later, as the mind becomes more cognizant of this turmoil passing through its matrix, it says "I" to this reaction and assigns it a familiar name. It is given a label drawn from the conditioned content of our own past experience of similar states.

For instance, have you ever heard within you, not necessarily in words, something to the effect of "Oh no, not this again!" Perhaps we're looking at the latest flame of our heart and we see a fire in his or her eyes, but it's not because they are looking at us. In that moment we no longer see the moment unfold *as it is*, but rather we stand there transfixed—experiencing the moment *as we are*; and we are not really present! We are back in our past, caught up in waves of emotional pain born of having become identified with other unhappy moments in our lives like the one unraveling before us. So, we are not really so much alive in the Now as we are reliving who we once were; and it is from our unconscious identification with this familiar flood of negative sensations that we derive a false sense of I. In this state of Self all sorts of runaway reactions rule us. Who hasn't wished there were some way to take back the angry words or cruel actions of this false self that literally sets itself on fire as it blames another for its pain?

What we want to learn from ongoing dramas such as this is that no false sense of "I" can run its self-compromising game on us without there being a *reason* for it—a reason our own mind provides by unconsciously calling up, and then identifying with, old negative images taken from some darkened closet of the past. If we can see that any step this false "I" takes to protect itself from the pain it feels only serves to make it, and the pain it is experiencing, seem more real, then we can see why this fictitious self has to go.

The next time (and every time) you catch some negative thought or feeling that says, "I am anxious," "I am scared," "I am mad," or "I am in so much pain"—the *first* thing to do is to come wide awake to yourself. By taking the following inner action, you can deliberately snap yourself out of that dark dream that is trying to weave itself into your identity. Rather than allowing yourself to be drawn into all the reasons that have appeared in your mind to justify why you should cry, reach instead for the shelter of the present moment. Then, while knowing that this negative state is present and pressing you to identify with its little life, work as consciously as you can to drop everything in that negative declaration except for the awareness of I *am*.

In other words, let go of any dark definition of yourself about to be draped over you. Just stand there, in the Now, within the light of your awareness and allow your newly awakened state to give you its identity. Then be still; just watch. Be the new you that sees the moment as it is—instead of being deceived into seeing what that false I wants you to see so that it can go on stealing your life!

Your awareness of these troubled thoughts and feelings roaming through you is the power that keeps their harmful and self-limiting influences from having control over you. Their aim is to get you to define yourself by identifying with their dark and defiling energies. Your aim is to remember that who you really are cannot be confined by dark thoughts or feelings any more than the light from a bulb can be contained in its glass.

As with all true spiritual exercises, we must approach them with great intention and persistence. The habitual dark states that have been misguiding us up to now will not give up their place at the steering wheel of our soul without struggle. Never mind any setbacks that you may experience as you put forth these new inner efforts. Whenever you find yourself a captive in the dark little kingdom of some unkind, troubled thought or feeling, just remember right then your wish *to be*. Drop whatever would define and limit you by bringing yourself back into the great and unconditioned Now where all is one. That's your part. The truth will handle the rest.

UNCOVER THE FOUNTAIN
OF FRESH STARTS HIDDEN IN YOU

We tell ourselves that we want a new life; in our minds we see our-selves reclaiming our right to live without limitations. We see our-selves walking away from destructive relationships and letting go of negative thoughts and feelings. And this is the very problem. We talk to ourselves about a fresh start and even plan the path we will take *when things get right* . . . but that's it. We think, but rarely act. We dream, but won't awaken to the one fact we must face *if* we would make a fresh start: *The new beginning we long for is now or never.*

There is no such thing as tomorrow for anyone who really has it in his or her heart to start over with life. There is only one place where we can hope to make a fresh start in life, and this has to be in that place where life itself is new all the time. But before we discuss where this fountain of fresh starts is found, we must grasp what may be a challenging idea: the true place of all new beginnings—the only one where it is possible for us to begin our life over anew—is, in reality, neither a *place* nor a *time.*

This thought may seem a bit confusing at first but, by calling on personal experience, we can confirm the truth of it. All of us know those high hopes we have that a new relationship, or change of career, will give us a new starting place in life. But we also know, at best, that these times and places in our lives are more like the momen-tary burst of a skyrocket than a permanent star on the horizon. And when the sizzle fizzles, we are right back where we started from, look-ing to change another set of conditions and calling this a fresh start.

As long as we look for some person or a point in time as the starting place for where we will make our new beginning, we cannot succeed. What is genuinely new is not personal, physical, temporal, or otherwise conditional at all. Such places that we long for are little more than illusions, creations of one's own desire trying to douse its own fires. And this is just the point: these longings for a fresh start are promise-driven, but powerless to deliver us to where within us a new life begins. This brings us to a key lesson.

The home of the new does not begin in the fading fires of the old; it is not a continuation of passing time or creature, but the secret ground from which these conditions arise. This teaches us that what is truly new begins only as the end of something is reached, a finding that calls to mind the myth of the fire-feathered phoenix resurrected out of dead ashes—a timeless image that amplifies the teaching that Real Life is never merely a continuation of what has been. This discovery that we must lose what *was* before we can have what *is* has meaning beyond what words can describe, but one of the ways we can apply this insight to our everyday life might look like this:

We cannot *plan* a fresh start in life; if we want a new life we must do something new. We must act in the Now . . . beginning with calling upon the light of our new understanding to go before us. Here is what this means to us in practical terms:

The fresh start we seek appears only as our old self disappears— only as we willingly die to who we have been. There are any number of ways to state this venerable wisdom, but the action required remains unchanged: If we wish to start our lives over new, the spiritual price is that we agree to no longer carry over our thoughts about ourselves from moment to moment. To this end, and to help us do what is needed to free ourselves, we need to see that while our habit of revisiting and then reliving past mental and emotional states may lend us welcome and familiar sensations, it also costs us our chance to know the newness of Now where our True Self resides in a state of natural peace and power.

The deliberate work of walking away from one's past is a prerequisite for recovering one's True Nature. But the false self will not sit quietly by as we work to break its hold on us. It may profess otherwise, but its dark nature loathes the light of Now because it is unable to enter into its newness. After all, how can it? You might as well try to take a shadow into the sun's corona! This thought-driven desire machine only knows itself by calling up and then considering its own images of past experiences. But in the living Now there are no well-worn images of former glories or future lights—only the Spirit of New Life itself.

As we work to be in the Now and strive to leave the old thought-self behind us, it will cry out something like this, "But you can't live without me! Who will watch out for you and see to your well-being if not me?" And though it is necessary that you learn to craft your own answer to this trickster nature, this one is the enemy of all that is fresh, uncorrupted, and new. Here is one response worth remembering. Send this message out from your silently seeing heart to this deceptive foe of all fresh starts in life:

"What I need, you cannot give me. What I long to see, you cannot show me. And what I hope to be, you cannot make of me. This conversation has reached its end."

Then, remaining as awake to yourself as you can, just keep walking ahead into the new and unknown Now. You need remember only one thing as you go: if you keep the light of your new understanding before you at all times, those shadows that would keep you from making a new beginning will remain behind you. Let this truth be your guide and watch how easy it becomes to let go of all that *was* in favor of all that *is* new, true, and you.

FIVE WAYS TO RAISE YOUR LEVEL OF SPIRITUAL FREEDOM

Picture in your mind a large mining operation, and just outside the opening to the mine, lined up for quite a ways in front of the pay-master's table, are a number of people waiting to collect their bimonthly paychecks. Somewhere in the middle of this line stands a man dreaming of the dollars about to come into his hands. As he waits he envisions all the things he will be able to buy with this money, and the imagined treasures and pleasures make waiting in line almost too much to bear. At last his turn arrives. He steps up and holds out his hand.

As he extends his hand for the check he believes due to him, the paymaster checks his log, looks up at him, smiles, and says softly so as not to offend: "Excuse me sir, perhaps you have forgotten. This line is only for people who have worked the last two weeks, which you did not. Surely you don't expect to be paid for something you haven't done, do you?"

The moral of this story is simple: the freedom our heart longs for isn't free, any more than a breathtaking view from high atop a mountain can be experienced by someone standing on the valley floor. Yes, of course the view is free, but only once we do the work of reaching that place wherein such natural beauty dwells.

Here are five proven ways you can learn to work in the Now to ensure that you reach ever-higher levels of personal freedom. However, this set of spiritual exercises requires a bit of special explanation, for not only will they prove themselves productive in terms of help-ing you to let go and live in the Now, but also each of these lessons is intended to work as the seed of a meditation.

The list that follows holds unique insights into the lofty nature of that rare individual who has found what all of us are looking for: unconditional freedom. Our honest examination of these spiritual assertions—based upon our own life experience—proves our need to realize their promise. For best results first meditate on what each statement means in and of itself. Let the freedom it illustrates awaken in you the remembrance of that part of you that knows its inherent truth. Then, consciously allow your mind to contrast your present level of freedom with that of the example you just meditated upon. By this practice you will see that each of these statements is seeded with an implied spiritual practice, a work meant only for you that you alone can *read* due to your present condition. With these thoughts in mind there is one other important point to remember.

Our intention in this exercise is not to create a set of pleasing self-images for us to go out into the world and imitate. All forms of imitation are spiritually disastrous. Nor should we allow any part of us to sit in judgment of us, all too glad to point out how badly we have missed the mark. Our sole task is to increase the consciousness of ourselves. That's it. This awakened awareness, the Living Light within us, working in concert with the self-knowledge it has helped to seed in us, not only reveals what stands in the way of our true freedom, but also sets the stage for its removal as well.

1. We are spiritually free when we no longer want anything to do with sitting in judgment of others, regardless of their perceived transgression. We realize that we live in an intelligent universe whose unerring system of justice ensures that no act—good or evil—goes unrewarded.

    Implied Exercise: Learn what it means to leave those who would punish you with word or deed to the bitter fruit of their own designs. Let go of the judge in you by recognizing we cannot hold someone's feet to the fire without suffering getting burned ourselves.

2. We are spiritually free when we never again feel envy for any other human being because of their position or possessions in life. We understand that regardless of external appearances, the quality of

our life experience is not determined by what we may or may not possess, but only by what we have allowed to take possession of our heart.

Implied Exercise: Catch and drop any part of yourself that wants you to think about yourself relative to others by comparing yourself to them. This dark nature doesn't care what it costs you to serve its insatiable appetite for dissatisfaction. Serve your True Nature instead by choosing to remember that who you really are is incomparable.

3. We are spiritually free when we never again allow ourselves to get caught up in some mad rush, regardless of what seems at stake. We know that wherever we are, whatever the circumstances surrounding us, we are always in the right place at the right time to further our relationship with the Divine.

    Implied Exercise: It is never what we are in a hurry to win that makes us real winners in life. Real victory is always the discovery that we can't give ourselves away to negative states and experience a positive outcome. Detect and reject any feeling that wants to put its rush on you. Do this by realizing that your True Nature awaits you within, so where is there to get to in such a hurry?

4. We are spiritually free when not one part of us harbors any hatred or resentment for any other human being, regardless of how badly that person may have once treated us. We have seen for ourselves that giving any dark state of hatred or resentment any reason to exist is the same as supplying it with a hidden refuge in ourselves.

    Implied Exercise: Once we can understand that everything we resist in life increases its weight by the magnitude of thought spent not wanting it, then we realize that it isn't our enemies who are burdened by those black wishes we hold for them, but it is we who are held hostage in the darkness of our unenlightened self. To see that it is hatred that hates is to let it go.

5. We are spiritually free when we have no fear of shouldering those moments when life brings more challenges than we have ever had to handle before. We understand the spiritual law that holds we cannot be harnessed to any load without being given the subsequent strength we need to succeed with it.

    Implied Exercise: Always accept a little more responsibility whenever conditions in life ask you to step up and test your spiritual strength. Just as our willingness to risk failure is one of the prerequisites for learning to live without fear, so too is our willingness to reach the end of our power an invitation to realize a source of a power within us without end.

The next and last five lessons in this chapter's section are higher insights rarely discussed among the spiritually uninitiated because of the measurable effect that their strong medicine causes in the soul. But I have chosen to include these teachings because not only do they help summarize our prescription for a free life, but they also present the case for why we need such a healing. Welcome these truths into your mind and watch how their refreshing view of reality leads you to that unconditional freedom for which your heart longs.

1. To weigh the value of what this world can reward us with, we need only remove the scales from our eyes; for were we willing to measure how many times we have fallen victim to a world that promises us victory, then we would know just how hollow is the hope of finding treasure in a bottomless basket.

2. If common social convention—with all is contrivance and hypocrisy—has one redeeming value, it is this: the happy day may come when we realize that most of our lives have been spent conversing with clever thieves, making plans with unseen liars, and listening to promises of people who are, by majority, incapable of a single act of integrity. This day of our awakening is the same

as the delightful date of our departure from a bankrupt world filled with beggars dressed as kings and queens.

3. Billions give their lives away for a moment's pleasure or for the promise of approval. They sacrifice their happiness in the hope that by acquiring power they can make their world a prettier place in the face of all the ugliness that these same pursuits create. The few and the true also give their lives away, but in acts of quiet selflessness that naturally follow the footsteps of those who have preceded them on the upward path.

4. For anyone with ears to hear there is but one question and one answer: Will we wait patiently for a single moment of relationship with what is eternal and real, where, with the touch of something timeless, all the moments of our life are forever changed? Otherwise we waste the few moments of our life chasing the pleasure of an imagined time to come that forever recedes from our grasp in the same instant that we reach for it.

5. No one can say no to this world who is afraid to walk through it alone. The unseen cost of this baseless fear is not just ending up in the company of cowards, but that one may lose the possibility of ever coming to know the company of the Divine.

ASK THE MASTERS

QUESTION: Why must we spend so much time giving ourselves over to working for our spiritual freedom? After all, I know of at least one conventional religion that says all we have to say is, "I believe in you," and we are free!

ANSWER: *It is said God created man free. That is a great misunderstanding. Freedom cannot be given to anyone—even by our all-loving Creator himself. God has given to man the biggest thing he can—that is, the possibility to become free. The desire for freedom exists in every man worthy of the name— but people are stupid, and they think they can have outward freedom with-*

out inner freedom. All our evil comes from this stupidity. Unless we desire, first of all, to be free from our own inner enemies, we shall only go from bad to worse. —G. I. Gurdjieff

QUESTION: I am getting the distinct feeling from my studies of spiritual truth that I need a whole new education. Is there one path or another that will make a better beginning?

ANSWER: *True education is to learn how to think, not what to think. If you know how to think, if you really have that capacity, then you are a free human being—free of dogmas, superstitions, ceremonies—and therefore you can find out what religion is.* —J. Krishnamurti

KEY LESSONS IN REVIEW

1. You have a secret feature of yourself that cannot be dominated by a dark thought or fearful feeling any more than a crashing ocean wave can crush the life out of a ray of sunlight.

2. Life itself has never weighed so heavily upon us as to hurt us; rather it is we who—in ignorance of reality—carelessly attribute weight to events that are essentially without substance, causing ourselves to suffer nothing less than the fervent magnitude of our own imagination.

3. True freedom is within what I am, not in what I have. If I have not this freedom of being free in what I am, then any other sense of freedom becomes my unseen captor, only posing as my liberator.

4. We are not held captive by anything in this life except for those relationships we consent to that are created out of our mistaken and unconscious belief that who we are—our God-given being— is not enough in itself. With this idea in mind, here are two spiritual laws that can help lead us to realize liberation:

* It is a law that there is always something higher for us to see whose expanded view instantly grants us greater freedom, and that these successive new heights have their secret home within us.

* It is a law that all things good come to those for whom the good is all things. There can never be any real negative consequence to any positive effort that we make to grow beyond our present limitations.

5. The fear we feel that we can't succeed or start life all over again is because our old nature wants us to believe that the path to a new self requires that we retrace our steps and fight our way back to an unsoiled starting place in life. But here's the truth: There is no pathway, past or future, that leads to real self-newness. The secret place of all fresh starts in life unfolds right from where we are, here, in each moment that we will dare to leave who we have been behind us.

CHAPTER FOUR

Let Go and Know the Peace of Now

Have you ever watched a mother hold her new child, or seen a doe gently nuzzle her fawn as it stood there balancing on uncertain legs? Did you ever stand outside in the still air washed clean by the passage of a spring storm, or feel yourself moved by the sight of tall trees swaying in a summer's breeze? Maybe your imagination has been caught and held still as you stood looking out over a rugged seacoast, or you've found your attention willingly arrested by some late-afternoon light whose colors made heaven seem not so far away.

All moments like these share a quality of quietness that is timeless, even as they whisper these traits to us in the perfectly present Now. And for those of us fortunate enough to hear these secrets, we know that more is gleaned from them than words may portray. Reasons for this truth abound, but one rises above the rest: the silence of such stillness is golden because it is uncorrupted; its quiet presence within us enlarges us because through our communion with it we are entered into a relationship with the peace of a vital Now beyond the reach of time. With these thoughts in mind, let me introduce you to a living stillness that dwells in the secret heart of you. Together we will explore the life of this higher reality. Let our discoveries prove to be the invisible ground that is one and the same as our True Self!

Some time ago, books with "magic" pictures in them became a popular fad. Each book was filled with page after page of complex, colorful, computer-generated graphics. The claim of the publisher was that if one knew the "secret way of seeing" then he or she would be able to see into the magic pictures and discover secret images hidden in them. A visual treasure hunt! Who could resist?

Upon first glance, the pictures were nothing more than a mad mishmash—drawings filled with diverse colors and a collision of designs that looked like they were created by a child run wild with crayons. However, if viewers could focus their eyes in a certain way and then hold them in the right place on the page before them, the confusion of crazy colors would somehow fade away to reveal a beautiful 3-D image hidden within them in plain sight! The magic in these pictures was that one could not hope to see the magic in them using one's usual way of seeing. Now for the connection we have been working to make.

Just as the amazing pictures in these magic books would seemingly appear from the depths of nowhere once one learned the secret of seeing through the chaos of colors, so too the peace of the perfectly present moment, in which dwells the kingdom of heaven, sits in plain sight in the midst of the chaotic content of our lives.

This full peace, which we might also call stillness or perfect silence, is what our heart of hearts longs to know. Within it there is neither stress nor sorrow. Yet, while most of us agree we seek a way to commingle in the Life of this deep quiet, its timeless realm remains all but imperceptible to us. Here is the reason why: it is a curious spiritual fact that we don't see stillness, even though it acts as the backdrop for all motion. This fascinating fact deserves a moment's consideration.

Of course, we can see things themselves, various creatures, even one's own thoughts and feelings moving across and through this still backdrop of life. And yet the condition we remain effectively blind to is this: if it weren't for the invisible backdrop of perfect stillness, of pure peace, we would not see any of these forms in the manner that we do!

A moment's study of a short analogy will take us a long way. If we went to a cinema expecting to see a story unfold, complete with movie stars, scenery, action, and interaction, but there was no screen there in the theatre to act as a backdrop for the projection, the showing of that movie would be meaningless. One would see no more than a whirl of indistinguishable light and phantomlike motions projected onto the various protruding walls guarding the way to the back of the stage.

Can we begin to see, in this instance, how the movie screen—that silent backdrop of white stillness that reflects the projected images—is equally essential to our understanding of all the activity that we see displayed upon it? Can we begin to see how without the former in place as a constant, the latter has virtually no context and therefore no real consequence? Now let's carry this idea over to see the following truth in parallel: much in the same way as the screen in the theatre makes it possible for us to see the action-packed motions of the movie, it is an unseen stillness that reveals what we experience as being the ceaseless movement of life.

With this insight in mind, can we recognize how unaware we are at present of this abiding stillness in which we ourselves move and live? Furthermore, can we see that it's not that this stillness isn't there—it is! The fact is, it is we, ourselves, who are not present to this unchanging presence! This is a helpful discovery for us to make. Through it, we are able to see that everything that concerns our relationship with fundamental peace depends upon where we place and hold our attention from moment to moment.

A quick review of these last few facts reveals much about our present level of consciousness. At this stage of soul development, we are fairly well caught in the up and down motions of life. So distracted are we by these cycles of pleasure and pain that few of us are aware of the perfectly still kingdom through which our lives and their events run their daily course. These findings not only speak for themselves, but they also hint to us of another way to live. And, as we will see, such wisdom is the voice of the very peace we seek.

WHAT THE WISE ONES WANT US
TO KNOW ABOUT THE NOW

All through the ages the Wise Ones have spoken of an invisible kingdom—a timeless ground known as the Now—that will confer to those who realize it a *peace that surpasses all understanding*. But what should be apparent from our study is that this peaceful kingdom is not really hidden; its quiet reality awaits us just out of sight of our present understanding, which further explains why there is no substitute for higher self-knowledge. If there's one great spiritual lesson it's this: we see everything about this life of ours through the eyes of our understanding of it, and the further this kind of seeing goes, the deeper runs one's being.

Fortunately, as this next short writing helps to explain, we are not left only to our own devices when it comes to realizing our latent possibilities. To span the distance between our present self and what is possible for us to become, we have a secret friend whose sole task is our spiritual fulfillment.

TO BREACH THE ABYSS

No action begins apart from
His Stillness,
The mind quieted sees this
And bears within it
A winged wish; a dark chrysalis
Waiting on a Living Light
To break the silence . . .
That beckons it, Leap!
Fly sorrow's joy!
Breach the abyss between this . . .
And that.

What does it mean to "breach the abyss between this . . . and that?" Here, we meet the idea of a new nature capable of breaking through the illusion of the opposites. We learn of an understanding that lives high above the perceived gulf between sorrow and joy, success and failure, even life and death. This stanza also hints to us about a certain level of ourselves that is caught up in the movement of life: an unenlightened nature that helplessly swings back and forth between up and down, pleasure and pain, from *this to that*.

Such interior knowledge of self has been taught in all true spiritual traditions of the East and West throughout all time. It is Christian, Buddhist, Muslim, Hindu, and Hebrew all at once. Truths like these help us to see that if we would be free we must transcend the opposites that blind us to the kingdom of peace by binding us to the world of passing sensation. And, with one last thought, it is worth mentioning here that the Bible verse attributed to Christ, "Wherever two or more of you are gathered in my name, there shall I be," relates directly to this new understanding and the grace born of it.

To continue our translation of this poem, freedom from these opposites, from the unconscious aspects of the soul whose natures oppose one another, begins with understanding that within each of us dwells a dark chrysalis. We may think of this chrysalis as being a kind of celestial seed that represents one's undeveloped soul. Its sleeping essence needs only to awaken in order to realize the vast potential it has to be one with peace itself. When the light pierces its darkened nature, when the Living Spirit stirs the latent spirit within this shell, the once-divided and conflicted soul is transformed and made whole. In that moment one becomes a reborn creature, now empowered by reason of its own new wholeness to *fly the abyss*.

What this means is that one's new level of being effortlessly transcends the opposites and takes its natural place in that timeless world of stillness, out of which all opposites arise. Shankara, the great Indian philosopher who founded the school of thought called Advaita Vedanta, reaches across the ages to confirm our findings: "This state of silence is a state of entire peace, in which the intellect ceases to occupy itself with the unreal. In this silence, the great soul who knows and is one with Brahma (the Creator) enjoys unmingled bliss forever."

So very much rests upon realizing our True Nature.

No one can hope to know the joy of true personal freedom without knowing the truth of spiritual peace. Freedom and peace are as kite and wind; the former remains grounded without the latter. This is to say that before we will feel ourselves being lifted above the conflict and illusions of this world, peace must become conscious within us. Peace is the foundation, freedom the form built upon it. We must never forget this relationship. To do so is to spend our lives searching for freedom through our relationship with worldly forms—an act that effectively builds prisons we then struggle to escape!

The next natural step in our study is to see that if our peace is built upon worldly forms, then it will be, at best, a temporary peace. Things, people, places, conditions—these are worldly forms, and they are what most of us pursue to help erase the ache of having no peace in our hearts. If we wish to take the next step in our spiritual development, then we must be willing to acknowledge that the pursuit of these forms, even their possession, has never brought us anything but a fleeting sense of fulfillment. As we will learn, peace and its freedom are born in the stillness that reveals their true nature within us. This is why true peace does not belong to any culture, tradition, race, creed, or religion. Its nature transcends all temporary fashions and forms of time.

No one may convince another that this perfect peace exists. The very attempt to do so vexes not only those souls involved, but also proves that the one who feels the need to push his own version of peace is not in fact rooted in the peace he presents himself as having. One should be wary of people who are aggressive in the name of peace! Here are a few good reasons why:

True peace is not the effect of a pact. Neither can it be produced by any plan.

True peace never flowers in opposition to anything. Its goodness cannot be manufactured, even from the finest of parts.

True peace is not the possession of any person, group, or organization. None can grant another this peace. Those who claim to be its keeper only keep others from finding it.

BREAK THROUGH THE BARRIER
BETWEEN YOU AND TRUE PEACE

If we wish to find peace we must understand something of its life. Here are a few such facts: Peace is the natural radiation of a living Now; it is one with that Light whose life is the eternal present itself, even as the emanations of light and warmth are one with the sun from which they radiate. If our intuition can perceive that the above ideas are based in truth, then we should be naturally moved to ask the following question: If this peace we long for is inherent in this perfectly present moment we call the "Now," what is it that keeps us from knowing the fulfillment of its promise within us? Let's look.

Through even casual observation, we can see that the primary governing body of our present self seems to be a mental and emotional construct whose sole occupation in life seems to be an ongoing consideration of what was and what will be. This activity amounts to what we experience as an endless weighing of our past and subsequent planning of our future. Stated in another way, our lives are currently made up of what we name for ourselves as being good days or bad days. Of course these "good" and "bad" days are labeled as such based on how they measure up to our desired expectations. Good days "happen" when we get what we desire, and bad days are . . . well, you know!

Now, one of the strange features about this present nature of ours is that even on "good" days—when we manage to achieve what we desire and feel a sense of satisfaction—this conditional peace often turns against us; triumph becomes a kind of torment as we end up fearing we will lose the thing just gained. Poof goes our peace! There is no profit in it, and its promises are equally empty.

We have another nature, one whose life and whose peace are the same character. This order of Self, and the Now that is the backdrop of its being, are as the branch is to the life-giving vine. No true peace can survive apart from this relationship. Any other form of peace is its earthly expression. But to make the point: No order, no peace. Order is peace.

This peace confounds the lower level of mind that only knows stillness by what it imagines its qualities to be. The mind asleep to itself—and hence to the reality of the stillness spoken of earlier upon which life is seen dancing—cannot conceive how its own images of winning in life deny it the victory over life for which it longs. In order to know peace and its promise, we must release ourselves from this sleeping self that is always struggling to put pieces of peace together in the vain hope they will stay united!

We have all tried sewing pieces of peace together, thinking through what we must do to rid ourselves of whatever nags at us. You know the dialogue one is ever having with oneself:

"Hopefully this career change will make things better; maybe going to the gym will get my love life going; once I make him understand my point of view. . . ." "As soon as" becomes the chant and the source of our confidence. We all know how this goes. The chattering is as endless as one's fear of feeling empty. And the more of these "pieces of peace" we juggle, the more anxious we become, all the while hoping that life won't break up what we would assemble. Even though this approach has proven itself fruitless, still we cling to the hope that *next time* things will be different. What we must see is that our lives cannot change until *we* do—from the inside out.

To succeed in our quest, we need a new and higher understanding of our own being. For this peace that we seek resides within us; it is not to be found anywhere else, which leads us to the next step in our search. To enter the silent world of peace requires that we learn the secret of being still. We must discover and enter into our own still being.

The task before us is not an easy one, and anyone who tells you differently lies; but we are not asked to make this journey without a guide. Before us goes the Light of Truth. It reveals the Way by opening our eyes to see among other truths, that the peace we seek is not a thing created by us. We learn that admission into its celestial kingdom is by mutual consent only, even though this peace agrees to no terms other than its own. It makes the rules, not us. Yet we are eventually made grateful for these unyielding laws, for whatever soul agrees to bend its will to these terms of eternal peace not only finds

God's peace revealed, but also that this providence has now become a permanent presence within his or her heart.

DISCOVERING THE IMPERSONAL NATURE OF TRUE PEACE

As surprising as it may be to learn at first, part of our findings will prove to us that the more "personal" is our peace, the more punishment we are likely to attract from it! Sometimes the simplest things show the deepest truths: Have you ever been in the midst of that personal peace called, "sitting in front of the TV with a nice pizza"? You know what happens next! The phone rings or a neighbor drops by and . . . Boom! One's slice of heaven is replaced with simmering resentment toward the person or event seen as disturbing it.

Or how about that sense of peace found in a new romance? That is, until we realize that rather than our heart being rescued by our *newest* lover, he or she now holds it for ransom by always threatening to walk out on us! And don't we all know that sense of feeling peacefully complete just after we buy that special something we've always wanted? Too bad that the bill still has to come!

It isn't that there is anything inherently wrong with such contentment; the point here is as simple as it should be clear: the moments made up of this kind of personal peace never last. In fact, the more we try to shape our individualized heaven, and contrive to protect those things we think bring us peace, the more we are punished by the increasing realization that such a personal peace can never last.

Which brings us to a key lesson: true peace is impersonal. Its reality cannot be possessed. Whoever tries to claim it or otherwise contain it, sows into his or her self the secret cause of conflict and sorrow. Herein we can begin to see why it is that when people try to organize peace, we inevitably see conflict and war continuing in the wake of their efforts.

So can we see in each and all of these cases that peace herself is trying to educate the soul? And though she teaches us her ways perfectly, only few become wise. This is true because so many of us unknowingly discard her tutoring. Sadly, we have yet to become "teachable" by truth. A short review of where we refuse her instructions will help us to better see the light and how it waits on us!

For example, take any of those daily disturbances that course through us and have their way with us. We resist these little shocks with our whole being. Yet each and every one of them brings a needed life lesson to us. The problem is that we usually don't "hear" these silent teachings (of peace) because the noise of our own answers drowns out her voice. With a touch of hindsight we see that all of these lessons boil down to one instruction: "Stop! What you are doing does not work. Wake up! You're looking in the wrong place. This kind of pain does no one any good!"

If we could only become quiet enough to listen anew, we would learn that peace is a gift given freely to each of us, right where we stand. But it is a gift given only when we give up our position that it is in our power to *possess* peace, as we would all other desires.

Peace cannot be bound but must be let loose by our growing realization that only in willingly losing ourselves within its life can we hope to know its everlasting tranquility. And yet, even though this peace cannot be bound, neither can it be lost! If you ever feel that you have lost peace, you must look to see where it is that you unknowingly, in error, gave it away or set it down by identifying with disruptive dark thoughts and conflicted feelings.

As you embrace these new ideas, if you find some value in them, then quietly ask yourself this all-important question: "How important is it for me to know peace?" Please be assured that we cannot ask ourselves this question often enough, and here is why: every time we seriously ponder the place of peace in our life—its real worth, what it really means to us—we are really wondering, "*What is it in my life that really matters?"* A short list, common to most of us, more than illustrates the point.

Is it power I want so that I can feel in control of my life and its desires? Most of us answer: "Yes, that's what I want."

Or wealth? Won't riches and more personal possessions give me a sense of security in the midst of this world that seems to be teetering on the brink of madness? Most of us think: "Yes, that only makes sense! Besides, why not!"

Wouldn't it be nice to find another special relationship to keep me from feeling lonely, to assure me that I am someone worth loving? "Yes. Yes. Yes!"

The bottom line is twofold: First, our present nature continues investing itself in various relationships that, at best, provide us a nervous peace. Second, we do not want to see this fact, which explains why, as a rule, we look away from the light that reveals the truth about these fleeting, unfulfilling desires. We submit ourselves instead to the will of a deceptive self that believes that rewrapping garbage is the same as throwing it out! We can do so much better, but our success requires that we become more inwardly discerning, as this next insight reveals.

If we look closely, the following will become self-evident: There is something at work within us that is stealing our peace; *there is a thief of peace among us.* Our glad task is to unmask its cunning nature.

To help set the record straight, and to ensure that we reach the right conclusion, haven't we assumed most of our lives that this "thief of peace" was that insensitive person who hurt us, that memory from our past that still causes us pain, or that hope that was shattered by an uncooperative event? Of course, this is the way we see it! As human beings we form relationships and then, when the form or dynamic of these relationships change, as they must, we blame these unwanted changes for our loss of peace. Such behavior is like getting mad at the wind that catches our hat and whisks it away.

Our sense of lost peace, along with feeling the loss of one's freedom that was tied to it, has never had anything to do with peace withdrawing or withholding its goodness from us. What we must see is that such a sense of loss is inescapable as long as we accept the limitations of our present nature as being the extent of our possibilities. Its only peace is a derivative one—a borrowed sensation taken by identifying itself with passing forms, be they things or thoughts about them. It is this level of self, and nothing and no one else, that is the thief of our peace.

The next time something dark or disturbing tries to steal into you to wreck your contentment, do not consent to be drawn into its seemingly important considerations. Instead of sinking into this yawning abyss, rather than running after something to resolve that rift, better to remember this truth: *the peace you long for also longs for you.* Then, whatever you must do, find your way to it!

Here's a good place to start. It is the first step into stillness: watch for, and then catch the thief in the act.

What does this mean?

As we discussed earlier, come awake to the backdrop of stillness within you, and while being aware within it, watch your own thoughts and feelings trying to drag you into the noisy world of their worry and fear. If you will go silent before them, they have no choice but to enter into the silence with you. This is how we turn the table on these thieves of peace. They cannot live with you in the light of Higher Self-awareness. In this mansion there is room for only one. You can work at this exercise anytime you remember it. Lay down your book and try it now.

PRACTICING THE PRESENCE OF PEACEFULNESS

Look past the familiar forms around you, including those reactions in you about them. Don't *think* about the moment unfolding before you, *see* it; Be the whole of life in the perfectly present moment. This Now is where the Spirit of Peace resides. Drop the minutiae, the too-familiar sense of self found in sorting through the particular. Place your attention in the awareness of your thoughts instead of losing yourself within them and what they tell you is happening.

As you make these interior efforts you will no doubt hear your own thoughts tell you that what you ask is impossible, that you can't hope to succeed at separating the darkness from the light. To disarm any such disturbance in you, you need only ask yourself one thing: what else would you expect bats to tell a farmer who intends to pull down the dark and useless barn in which they live?

The thought that nature does not know its own captive state any more than a barnacle on a boat knows that it can't move itself from the hull of one ship to another. Its darkened nature can only imagine freedom—never know it. But our True Nature is created to know the very movements of heaven within itself, which is why we need to discover what is working within us that has us so anchored in time and space. Perhaps the analogy that follows, a simple situation common to us all, will help us better see into our present situation as well as show us how to escape its hold.

Have you ever sat in your living room with sunlight streaming through a window and seen, suspended in the light, all of those thousands of dust particles? If it helps, imagine this scene now. Before you, actually all around you, is this light. Within it, suspended, are countless tiny particles of dust. Now, with this image in mind, what is it that we look at?

Our attention is drawn to the dancing particles, while the light that makes these particles visible to our eye remains invisible in and of itself. Here is the reason for this: we don't see the light that makes it possible for us to see the particles because our present nature only knows itself in relationships that are based upon "particularity." It is only conscious of individual forms instead of their relationship to the whole. The inherent limitations of this level of self have become our lamentations. But it need not remain this way.

Within each of us, in our hearts and in our minds, there lives a special kind of light. In truth, it is everywhere. And to carry the last analogy a bit further, we can look at our thoughts as particles suspended in a silent, illuminated space. But, as we are learning, instead of seeing the beautiful stillness—the source of that which reveals the movement of these passing thoughts and feelings—we grab onto each thought that passes through it. Why would we do this? We are now close to the discovery of a great truth.

It is not the real you, not the real "I" in us that latches onto these thoughts. It is the thief of peace! This is our divided nature. It cannot live without that familiar sense of self that it forms each time it examines and evaluates the images it can sink its mental teeth into. In a word, this thieving nature that steals our peace is part and parcel of our blindness to the fact that real peace doesn't come in parts. Said slightly differently, the stillness we long for can never be found in any temporary sense of self that comes from being identified with the movement of one of these suspended parts. Again, this understanding is not a complex affair, so let's look at another example.

One reason why negative states sneak in so easily to steal our peace is that we have been conditioned to believe in their right to punish us. Here is proof of this dark conspiracy:

We can be seated at a nice quiet table in a restaurant, have enough money to buy a fine meal for ourselves, have on nice clean clothes, be by ourselves or with friends, and for all of our good fortune, we will get upset because the waiter didn't bring our toast buttered on the right side! As silly as this may sound, it's true: Negative states such as these, born of nothing other than conflict-filled, comparative thinking, steal into us to squander our peace one hundred times a day.

We do not have to yield ourselves to such meaningless states, nor live the life of the sorry self that revels in them. But emancipation will take a special effort on our part.

Following is a list for special Self-study to help get you started up the path of spiritual freedom. After a careful review of these peace-stealing conditions, take time to make a list of your own. Keep it simple. Use casual observations of yourself and others around you to be a spiritual detective.

UNMASK THE THREE THIEVES OF PEACE

1. One of the first thieves of our peace is spending time thinking about what others are thinking about us. Can we see that the only reason we are concerned with what others may be thinking about us is due to an imagined fear that they may have some power to take away what we are clinging to for our equally imagined peace? Let go! No one has the power to take peace away from you. It isn't theirs to give!

2. Another thief of peace is building a "case" against anyone for any reason. No one can steal our peace, so finding fault with another for how we feel is like falling asleep under the sun and then blaming it for the burn we get! The only way we lose our peace is when we mistakenly identify with some painful thought that would draw us into its petty life. Let go of being little. Drop whatever you have been tricked into resenting and watch peace return to take its place.

3. And last but not least, another common thief of peace is trying to

measure ourselves. For instance, have you ever noticed how, most of the time, we cannot have a conversation with someone without walking away and measuring our own performance? Even walking through a supermarket we wonder whether people are looking at us or not, and then we act accordingly. Step out of these mental movies; their producer is the misery of self-measuring. Let go because you know that it's impossible to be self-conscious and also be at peace.

There are many other ways in which our peace is stolen, such as when we find ourselves caught up in the excited anticipation of something, good or bad, coming our way or in the endless comparison of our lives to those of others—friends and strangers alike! Hoping to find a sense of peace in any form of comparison or anticipation is like waiting for a dark, overhead thundercloud to rain sunlight. We must aim to be this honest with ourselves in each moment.

For extra benefit, and as a way to amplify the impact of these last lessons, take a piece of paper and write down on the top of it: "Known or Possible Suspects Who Are Stealing My Peace." Then make a list of those thoughts, feelings, habits, or beliefs you have that you think need closer observation. This simple exercise will help you to exorcise those inner thieves that are intent on stealing your contentment.

The short "truth tale" that follows is intended to help us learn two very simple, yet crucial spiritual lessons in letting go. Read it carefully. Within its story is hidden the secret place where peace and stillness reside as one.

A father once took his young daughter to a nearby old growth forest. He knew that the stillness and beauty of the massive trees would work their enchantment on her, as it had always done upon him. And he was right; her little heart was at home in the quiet depths of these ancient trees. All was well for the first several moments, but then something broke into the peace of the place.

As they walked farther into the forest, he could see that his daughter was becoming overwhelmed. She would be looking at a particular tree when the sun would pass behind a cloud, giving rise to a great shadow that would move through the woods. Everywhere dark shapes stretched out, as if to touch her, and then the light would shift, creating motion somewhere else. On and off went this shadow show, so that one minute she would be absolutely captured with enthusiasm for the beauty of the light, and the next minute she would be scared by the encroaching shadows.

As her emotional state escalated, her father realized that her limited understanding was not enough to correct the developing negative condition within her. And so, taking action before she became any more frightened, he took his little girl by the hand.

"Come on, sweetheart," he said, and they walked back out of the forest and headed for the place where he knew a special lesson awaited her.

They walked hand-in-hand for twenty minutes or so, got outside the trees, and climbed a gentle hill to its crest where they could get a panoramic view of the forest. They sat down on the edge of the little bluff together and quietly looked down on the woods spread out beneath them. What a magical sight!

The little girl saw dozens of shadows caused by the clouds as they moved beneath the sun, even as she saw that the sunlight passing over the crown of the forest would create tree shadows within the woods that reached out and then raced back into nothingness. She saw the whole of the forest and its invisible relationship with the world around it. Wordlessly, she realized that no event happened by itself. And most importantly, from her new vantage point, none of the things that had troubled her within the forest troubled her now. She grew very still. Peace returned to her. Her new view of reality had granted her this gift. From that day on, whenever they went to the woods, she was no longer afraid.

SEVEN INSIGHTS INTO TRUE SILENCE

We, too, have within us a new, higher vantage point—a very special part of ourselves within which we may be at peace regardless of what goes on around us. This yet-to-be realized state of ourselves may be called conscious self-awareness. Through its power, instead of being pulled down into painful identification with the passing shadows of life, we can discover a life in a peace far above the reach of any fear.

Let's review what we have learned so far. One thing should be clear about true peace of mind: Either we are at peace wherever we are—because this peace goes with us—or what we call our peace is a product of some pleasurable condition over which we have temporary command. In situations like the latter, though largely unconscious to us, we sense that our peace is conditional. We know that we must work to keep certain prevailing conditions in place in order to remain at peace. And this, of course, means that we will resist any movement that threatens our desired estate. Clearly such a tentative peace is not true peace at all, because it dwells side by side, in league with an unseen conflict that is a basic requirement of its very existence!

What does this insight teach us? True peace is never a sensation. Its hidden nature is the expression of a timeless stillness, a silence not born of, and therefore beyond, the play of the opposites. This silence cannot be possessed. As it cannot be gained, neither can it be lost, which means that whomever it embraces lives in a world free of fear.

What does this mean to us? True silence may be called upon, but as it is without cause, it always appears on its own, remaining only as it pleases its purpose. Nevertheless, one may court this stillness through a quiet wish to understand its life within one's own. For this reason, our moment-to-moment meditation becomes a revelation if we open ourselves to truth and listen to what it reveals.

Study the next "Seven Insights Into True Silence" and allow their understanding to reveal the secret home of peace within you. Ponder these truths. Quietly turn them over and over in your mind. Soon you will hear what cannot be told.

1. Just as true emptiness holds all things, true silence bears all things. Whatever is brought into this silence, whatever it touches, is gradually silenced . . . not by an act of domination, but through a peaceful integration of a lesser peace into a greater one.

2. True silence is an interior presence and not an exterior circumstance. Its peace has no opposite and is not created, which means nothing can act against it or serve to enhance its existence.

3. True silence cannot be cultivated, but the interior conditions that prohibit its presence, and our relationship to the peace within it, may be recognized and released, allowing us to realize the silence we seek.

4. True silence is perfectly empty of content and completely full of peace, without any contradiction between the two.

5. True silence is without preference, and as it neither rejects nor resists any condition, it is always at peace.

6. True silence doesn't have intelligence—it is intelligence of an order, which a divided mind cannot comprehend. Its peace surpasses all understanding.

7. If we wish for the presence and peace of true silence, then the great necessity of solitude should be as evident to us as the knowledge that any seedling must be left undisturbed, if it is ever to break out of its dark ground and live in the light.

Let all we have looked into together show you that there is a higher world and that this peaceable kingdom of Now dwells within you. Allow your heart to remind you what the mind so easily forgets: there is a peace. There is a shelter. There is a timeless place in each of us that no darkness can shatter or dispel. Make it your one intention to spend your time there. Prefer its ever-present company to that of any promise of peace to come, and watch how your life grows happy and whole in stillness beyond compare.

ASK THE MASTERS

QUESTION: My world is so busy it feels as though there just isn't time to learn all that I must. With so much competing for my attention and all of it seemingly so important to my life, when would be the best time for me to make these truths my own?

ANSWER: *Now or never! You must live in the present, launch yourself on every wave, find your eternity in each moment.*

—Henry David Thoreau

QUESTION: I could really use some encouragement because no matter how many teachings I search through, try as I might, I cannot find the peace I long for. Where am I going wrong?

ANSWER: *O thou that pinest in the imprisonment of the Actual, and criest bitterly to the gods for a kingdom wherein to rule and create, know this for a truth: the thing thou seekest is already here, "here or nowhere," couldst thou only see.*

—Thomas Carlyle

KEY LESSONS IN REVIEW

1. There is no worry so great, no anxious rush for resolution so strong, that these terrible twins cannot be taken up, reduced, and returned to their basic nothingness by a mind brought back into its native quietude. Learning to be still is not just the remedy for our self-wrecking states but proves to be their permanent cure.

2. Only what awakens us to our own immortality truly profits us. All else serves only to gently rock us into a fitful sleep in the stream of passing time.

3. Fear is what happens to us whenever we forget that the One who created us fears nothing. True courage is remembering this truth and then daring to act upon it in the face of a fear. There is no other cause of fear and no other true solution. Awareness of this truth awakens in us the action that sets us free.

4. We do not cease to exist when, having surrendered ourselves to the starlit depth of a dark night sky, all thought subsides; or when for the invisible touch of an unsought love, our heart is filled with a gentle stillness. Rather, it is only within moments such as these—when we are enabled to forget about ourselves—that it may be said we truly live!

5. It only seems as though there is something more important for you to do than to just quietly be yourself.

CHAPTER FIVE

The Higher Self-Understanding That Heals All Hurts

W hat do we need to do to rise above the limitations of our present understanding—limitations that, seen or not, play a role in our daily dose of heartache? The answer may surprise you! Truth teachings throughout the ages tell us that healing the hidden and hurting places in our heart begins with becoming conscious of them. We are taught that we cannot free ourselves of anything that we refuse to meet face-to-face. The great American philosopher and self-realized author, Ralph Waldo Emerson, confirms this spiritual fact:

> In regard to disagreeable and formidable things, prudence does not consist in evasion or flight but in courage. He who wishes to walk in the most peaceful parts of life with any serenity must screw himself up to resolution. Let him front the object of his worst apprehension, and his stoutness will commonly make his fear groundless.

What encouragement! But these words are more than merely motivational. The promise hidden in this powerful principle doesn't just leave us wanting the courage we need, far from it. Such truths invite us to see our lives through their eyes, where we are shown the existence of a fearless heart, free from all self-compromise. We catch sight of a warrior's way, where the favorable outcome of our struggle becomes certain the moment we choose to explore what is yet to be discovered within ourselves. But that's not all. These same truths hint of the greatest gift of all—not only the *possibility* of a liberated life, but the promise of it fulfilled. And all that is asked of those who would enter this bright new world is to embrace its reality within themselves. Let's look at what is involved in taking such a bold step.

A SPIRITUAL PRESCRIPTION FOR PERFECTING YOUR LIFE

Two men who have worked for the same company for years, and who share an office, are having a conversation over lunch. They are in the company cafeteria with other workers around them, who are also eating their meals. Bob watches his friend Joe reach into his briefcase and pull out a small bright-blue bottle, which he has seen in Joe's hand a number of times over the last ten days or so.

Joe seems content and is even humming to himself as he takes a fairly deep sip directly out of the bottle. Bob watches the action and, sensing it may be a good time to ask, fields a delicate question: "How is it going these days with you, Joe? Are you feeling any better? You didn't say much after last week's appointment with your new doctor." Not wanting to appear nosey, Bob made his last statement sound more like a question, hoping that Joe would offer him more information without having to be asked directly.

Joe finishes his swallow and smiles back at Bob, "Well, as you know, I've had this recurring pain that I just couldn't shake, so I went to see a few specialists. But soon it was evident to me that these guys didn't know their heads from their elbows." He continued his story, silently congratulating himself, "That's when I found the greatest doctor in the world and, would you believe it, he lives in my apartment building! I tell you he knew right away what I needed, and the whole thing was virtually painless!"

"Gee, that's good news," said Bob taking a bite of his sandwich. "He must have been something pretty special, because I have never seen you be so religious about doing anything, let alone taking medicine." Bob couldn't resist his next tongue-in-cheek comment. "I guess the prescription he gave you must have been just what the doctor ordered!" What happened next came as a complete surprise, because suddenly Joe's expression became very serious.

"To tell the truth, Bob," Joe lowered his voice while slowly turning his head left and then right to ensure no one was near enough their table to hear his confession, "I have seen hardly any improvement at all. I'm still suffering quite a bit!"

Somewhat confused by this report, Bob whispers back, "But I've been watching you for over a week now and you haven't missed one dose of that drug he prescribed for you." Then he thought through the last few sentences in their conversation and leaned forward in his chair to ask: "What are you doing with that stuff if it isn't helping you to get any better?"

Joe looks down at the bottle still in his hand, leans forward onto his chair too, and whispers through a strange smile, "Well, the truth is, while this medicine hasn't done much to heal what's hurting me, there is something about it that I like;" and then he leaned even further forward and whispered, "You wouldn't believe how good this stuff tastes!"

There are many times when human beings are a study in stupidity. Just as we can see that distracting ourselves or otherwise concealing a pain has nothing in common with healing it, the same holds true in our relationship with self-wrecking states: more often than not our tendency is to be self-deceiving rather than be self-studying—where instead of doing the necessary inner work of illuminating the still-darkened corners of our consciousness, we look for ways to escape the fears that breed there like ghosts in a haunted house. Why?

For one thing, through a host of social and cultural mandates, we have been conditioned to believe that not only must whatever we suspect is "wrong" with us be hidden from the world around us, but such imperfections must also be kept from ourselves as well. Such ideas serve nothing but the sickness they help to conceal. Here is a guide to the real medicine.

SIX EYE-OPENING INSIGHTS TO START TRUE SELF-HEALING

We are made to be self-correcting, so that each real correction effected in us elevates us above the dark and limiting influences we have been living under all our lives. Like moving from a hot desert to a cool mountain retreat, each discovery of what darkens our path in life moves us toward higher, happier ground. And though we may not yet understand how this works in us, each time we catch a glimpse of one of our character shortfalls, we do so by the grace of a Living Light—a latent force for perfection that lives within us. And this same Higher Intelligence asks us, by its very presence within us, to see ourselves in its light. Through its illumination we discover that it is not negative to see the negative in us since it is the perfectly positive that makes this kind of seeing into ourselves possible. But we must be good patients!

When it comes to seeing the truth of our lives, the late, great author Vernon Howard taught those who would listen that "The medicine is bitter, but it heals." If we would heal the hidden hurt in us then we must learn that the initial bitterness of self-truthfulness is the front-runner of our ultimate spiritual betterment. Our work is to concede to the bright prescription of higher self-honesty, regardless of how it tastes to us in those moments when we see ourselves as we are.

Following are six eye-opening facts. They reveal areas in our lives where many of us have lived with our eyes closed, vainly hoping that if we don't see something regarding how we go about our lives, then it won't be able to hurt us. But now we know better, which means that a brighter life is just ahead.

We close our eyes to the fact that:

1. Wherever we go and regardless of whom we meet, we still seem to run into the same conflicts and experience the same negative reactions.

2. We blame others for their insistence that we serve their interests, when the real pain in such moments is our own resentment over a cowardly inability to just say no.

3. In spite of all of the pain it causes us and others, we still believe that we know what it means to be a winner in life.

4. Just because we have mastered hiding some character fault of ours doesn't mean that it has stopped hurting those around us.

5. We would rather have the company of known liars and betrayers than have to go through life by ourselves.

6. Crying for ourselves out of self-pity doesn't change one thing about the nature of the self that is the secret source of all these tears.

For extra swift healing, study these friendly guides with the intention of welcoming in their light. Remember that authentic self-healing must begin with truthful self-seeing. Just as the rising sun dismisses our fears of imagined dangers hidden in the darkness of night, higher consciousness of any unwanted condition must precede its correction. For those who would be free, the choice must be to see. Now, here is one last important insight. It will help keep you safe and strong throughout your entire journey as you uncover the undiscovered parts of yourself.

Whenever we see something in us that is cruel, selfish, or otherwise self-destructive, our first temptation is to hand ourselves over to another dark state called self-condemnation. Most people will tell you it feels natural to first judge and then loathe ourselves when we stumble over some secret ugliness in our heart. But we must avoid falling into this trap of secret self-torment. Its nature is actually self-torture. Here is how we succeed:

In these times of trial, we need only remember that the Living Light never shows us anything in ourselves that it hasn't already started to change for us — if we will only let It! This is the hidden meaning behind that timeless spiritual instruction "Let go and let God." Now let's gather some more encouraging truths.

If one day you bang your elbow and seven years later the same spot still aches, and now radiating pains are appearing in your fingers and shoulder, you would start to suspect that something in your body's system was amiss! You would conclude, virtually beyond any doubt, that your original injury never healed properly.

Now, such a simple injury rarely, if ever, becomes a complex physical problem for one simple reason: should the pain of the initial accident persist for longer than a few weeks, most people would realize that this has become an unnatural pain. As a result, most people would then seek professional diagnosis and treatment. Common sense tells us this, but now let's look at why this is true.

To start with, and by the very fact of its continuing presence in our body, we intuitively know that such pains are not supposed to linger on and on. But speaking of a pain that won't go away, that spreads and compromises other parts of the self, what about that ache that appeared that day your close friend betrayed your trusting heart? And what of other similar pains? What about that moment when our hopes were shattered by the collapse of a lifelong dream? Or that searing stab of pain that passed through us when our gift of love was rejected and summarily trampled on? Why doesn't it seem odd to us that these pains should persist and, in some cases, worsen as they so often do?

The real question before us is twofold: we have to ask ourselves not only why these types of mental and emotional wounds never stop hurting us, but also why it is that their hidden cause—that "slash" somewhere in our soul—just won't heal. And that's not the end. Most of us avoid, at all costs, receiving a similar bump in life, because we know how tender that first wound still is. After all, who wants to start the crying cycle all over again!

Once we collect even a few of the necessary facts, the answer to these reincarnating aches becomes obvious. Not only haven't we healed from these blows that life deals us—healings that ought to occur effortlessly and naturally under higher law, regardless of the psychic nature of the injury—but we've actually been resisting that which would help us heal.

Consider this: By the very absence of the healing that ought naturally follow any form of injury, we should be able to deduce that certain counter forces must be at work within us. There have to be unseen anti-healing forces with a vested interest in our continued suffering. If we can see the truth of this startling fact then we should also realize how vital it is for us to shed light on this unseen enemy of natural healing. Such insight is not just necessary, it is critical if we going to be able to help ourselves realize a true self-healing.

FULFILL THE HIGHER PLAN
FOR HEALING WHATEVER PAINS YOU

Let's begin this investigation with a simple illustration. Imagine for a moment the familiar pain that comes with having eaten ice cream too quickly, when one's mouth or throat gets that painful freeze feeling. When we experience a pain like this, we don't worry about what to do because, in this instance, we know a certain truth about the nature of this pain that prevents us from getting embroiled in it. What is this truth?

We simply know that this pain will pass as soon as its cause goes away. We may hop around a bit, but we know better than to leap into fear, blame, or self-loathing. Yet, in sharp contrast to this natural wisdom, whenever we get handed a cold-hearted blow from someone or something in life, everything about how we handle such moments changes. Our pain, instead of passing with its cause, persists. And rather than healing, our hurt gets constantly refreshed with every remembrance of that initial moment. Why is this so? What is happening within us? Follow the next few ideas closely to see these truths at work in you.

First, as we now suspect, there is at work in us an undetected nature that will not allow the cause of our pain to pass so that the healing may take place. Can we see that we have parts of us that just won't let go of being angry with someone who got angry with us? But that's not all!

Can we also see that these same smoldering parts of ourselves would have us believe that being on fire is the best way to get over being burned? Of course! Once we bring such self-destructive behavior out into the light we can also see that these actions must be unconscious to us; no one would consciously harm him- or herself.

Any part of us trying to drag us into a heated stew over "who" or "what" should be blamed for our pain is secretly working to divide and conquer us. This spiritual fact cannot be overstated, nor should the understanding of its rescuing power be underestimated, which is why we will now bring light into this dark deception.

In that moment when we are thrown into emotional conflict,

regardless of its initial cause, the first step this in-the-dark nature takes to deceive us is to direct our awareness away from the actual hurt we feel. It accomplishes this mean feat by its second step: it misleads us into placing our attention on the enemy outside of us, that person or condition that it points to as being responsible for our pain.

Once this unconscious self has succeeded in dividing us up in this manner, we now have less than half the possible powers that we need to heal. And if this wasn't bad enough, the remaining forces of light needed for our healing are themselves now half compromised by subsequent negative reactions that tell us to lash out at whatever it is that has been blamed for our pain!

The next time any pain—be it an old familiar one, or an altogether new ache—pushes itself in upon you, come wide-awake to yourself and remember this last important step: Do not try to do one thing with any psychological pain that passes through you, other than to remain as awake as you can to its presence within you. Then, into this conscious self-awareness bring the following new understanding: this pain is not you but, in reality, constitutes a calling out from the injured part of you to a Higher Power to be healed. Your job is to see that the call gets through. Nothing more, nothing less.

If you will do your part in fulfilling this higher plan for healing what pains you—and agree to simply hold this hurt of yours in the light of your own higher self-awareness—then the healing you hope for cannot be denied and has, in some ways, already occurred. All you need to do is remain true to this principle as it works itself out within you. The rest is done for you.

KNOWLEDGE TO BE STRONGER
THAN WHATEVER SHAKES YOU

QUESTION: "I know in my heart that what you are saying is right, and it sure sounds great in principle; but there's no getting around it:

the distance between what I know to be true—and my ability to act truthfully in the moment needed—is too great. Try as I might, I cannot overcome what compromises me. What am I missing here?"

ANSWER: The struggle to overcome any unwanted condition in our lives can only be as successful as our understanding of the nature of what we are struggling against. A man with an ax may overcome an unseasoned piece of wood with several deft blows, but whoever would use force to try and chop a negative state down to size usually ends up nothing but worn out for his fight.

QUESTION: "Are you saying that we shouldn't fight for ourselves —that we ought to just let negative thoughts and feelings have their way with us?"

ANSWER: No, we must fight for ourselves; only we must make it the right kind of fight. This requires that we learn to call on the light that we've been talking about. A short explanation will take us a long way toward acquiring this new and needed understanding.

Ancient generals knew that a great deal of their wartime success depended on where they would engage their foe. This accounts for why so many battles were fought over possession of the high ground in the contested area. In our spiritual battles with negative states the same principle holds true for us. Only the *high ground* that we must take and hold isn't a hillside or mountaintop stronghold, it is our higher understanding of the nature of our "enemy." We overcome our interior troubles not by force, but by realizing the true nature of their character and by understanding our relationship with it.

The wonderful old Grimm's fairy tale of "Rumplestiltskin" is based on this little-understood spiritual secret. What was the power that helped the heroine win her struggle against the dark force that was trying to steal her first born, this fable's metaphor for our essential essence? In the end, the heroine vanquished the evil little elf by uncovering his true name. In spiritual terms, this means that the power that came into her hands wasn't her own; it was a gift born of discovering the secret nature of her adversary. This is our task as well. A short story will shed some empowering light on our quest to be stronger than anything that would try to shake us.

Walking down the airline passageway toward the exit with the rest of the departing passengers, Chelsea was trying to fight back a mounting fear. Maybe she should have waited for that nice steward who had told her he would be happy to show her off the jet, but she had decided that was for babies. Now there was nothing she could do except go with the flow. Her apprehension grew. It wasn't so much that she was only seven years old, or even that this was the first trip she had ever made without her mom and dad; the problem was she couldn't see a thing. Well, that's not altogether true.

In front of her, behind her, wherever she looked—was a tide of legs and differently sized carry-on cases all pressing her and forcing her to move along in the same direction as they were. She wondered where everyone was headed in such a rush; a moment later she found out for herself.

"Chelsea," a familiar voice penetrated the wall of people around her. She knew immediately who was calling her, and she walked as fast as she could in that direction. Then she heard it again, "Sweetheart, over here. Come this way, child."

And like a lighthouse beacon for ships lost in the fog, there was her grandpa smiling down on her. She ran to his side and jumped up into the rescuing shelter of his open arms.

"Welcome to Grandpa's part of the world," he said softly into the bunches of blond curls that covered her ears, "And boy oh boy," he pulled her back so he could see into her eyes, "are we going to have a good time, just you and me for five whole days." She giggled to confirm his excitement, and a moment later the two of them headed off to collect her bags.

It was probably because she had already taken in so many new impressions, plus the fact that she had never seen so much open space in all of her life, that during the car ride out to her grandpa's ranch Chelsea could hardly keep her eyes open. Then suddenly she was awakened by a sharp bump that lifted her little body an inch into the air above the car seat. It took a few seconds for her to remember where she was, but when she heard the reassuring sound of her grandpa's voice she knew things were okay.

"Sorry Sweetie," he said; "out here where I live we don't have much of a call for paved roads. So hold on, 'cause there's lots more bumps where that one came from." And with that, just like he always did, Grandpa found a way to have some fun. He put both hands on the steering wheel and, making exaggerated gestures with his arms, began driving the car like Mr. Toad's Wild Ride at Disney World. They were both still laughing when the car pulled up in front of a sprawling ranch house.

When everything finally stopped moving around her, a sudden stillness overcame her. Her mother had told her that Grandpa lived someplace she called "Big Sky Country," but she wasn't prepared for the sheer size of the world she had entered. Spread out before her in every direction were low rolling hills that seemed, in the distance, to pile themselves up together into towering white-capped mountains beyond which her eyes could not see. Her grandfather must have sensed what she was feeling.

"Maybe sometime tomorrow, if you feel up to it, we can take a horseback ride and see this country up close. How does that sound to you?"

"What time?" Chelsea shot back, indicating she couldn't wait.

"Well," he answered, looking up into the gray skies overhead, "if this approaching storm brushes by like it looks it will, then we can get started first thing in the morning after breakfast. Would that suit the young princess?" he said in mock servitude.

She nodded her most royal-like approval and, after gathering her travel gear from the backseat of the car, they went inside the house.

It wasn't too long after the sun had gone down that Chelsea went upstairs to her room, slipped into bed, and fell quickly into a deep sleep. Little did she know as she drifted off into her dreams that a great storm was taking shape outside her window, and that with its arrival would come a very special life lesson that only the lucky few ever learn.

There was no way for Chelsea to know what had just happened, but she had *never* heard such a sound before; and whatever the noise was, it was so powerful that it almost knocked her out of bed! Part low rumble and part explosion, it rolled on and on like a bowling ball crashing down an endless lane.

She sat up, immediately awake, partially petrified but ready to run at the same time—but where would she go? Her mind struggled to clear itself. This wasn't her bedroom. Where was she? "That's right," she heard herself think: "I'm at Grandpa's." Then she said his name aloud, "Grandpa!"

Then came another boom, and with this blast also came the brightest flash of light she had ever seen. In that moment every chair and lamp in the room seemed to jump to life; and then, as suddenly as they moved, they simply stopped, fading back into the dark background from which they sprang. She had never seen anything like this before! Her heart leaped in such a way she was afraid it would pop right out of her. Then came not one, but a pair of flashes. This time the super white light brought no sound with it at all. The quiet was deafening until it was replaced by the sound of confused thoughts pouring into her young mind.

"What's happening? What should I do?" But an intense peal of twin thunderings gave her the answer. All by itself her body lurched backwards against the back of the bed. Instinctively she pulled her blankets along with her and huddled under them, eyes closed tight, as she tried in vain to protect herself from her own mounting fear.

Chelsea was experiencing the first electrical storm of her tender seven-year-old life. She had no idea what was happening—which is why, in a period of less than three minutes, the summer storm that had broken across the Montana plains had formed a center in her as well.

All she could think of was wanting to be back home where things like this just didn't happen; but a moment later, even though she knew that she wouldn't see her own familiar bedroom, she opened her eyes. And there, standing in the doorway of her room, backlit by a hall light was the oh-so welcome sight of her grandpa.

"Wow!" he said. "Pretty scary, isn't it?" But she could see that he didn't look at all frightened, and this made Chelsea relax the choke hold she had on her blanket. She would have run over to his side but as he was already walking toward her, she just opened her arms and gladly accepted his outstretched arms as her new set of covers. He picked her up, blankets and all, and carried her out of the room and downstairs into the living room. The two of them settled into a large leather chair seated right in front of a huge picture window.

Just outside, much closer than Chelsea wanted to be, she could see not only the open range around her grandpa's place, but also the raging storm. She started to protest when there came another bright flash and huge boom. Wind-driven rain pelted the window and it sounded like thousands of fingers tap, tap, tapping on the pane. She tried to bury herself in his chest, but his hands gently held her back and turned her face upwards to meet his gaze. "Is this the first big storm you've ever seen, Chelsea?"

Unable to find her voice, she nodded in the affirmative. He smiled back at her and asked what she thought had to be the dumbest question she ever heard!

"What do you think of it so far?"

She answered this time by squishing her face up into the tightest ball she could, as though she had just taken some terrible tasting medicine. "I see," he said. "That bad, huh?" Chelsea relaxed her brow and opened wide her eyes as if to admit that maybe she had overreacted. They shared a short, but welcome laugh.

"Shall I tell you something I learned just after your grandma passed away?"

With this question he turned her around, squaring her up in his lap so that the two of them now sat looking out the big picture window. At first, she started to resist the move. She did not like the feeling of being so exposed to the flashes of light that had continued through their dialogue, but it felt safe enough, so she let go a bit and snuggled down in his lap as much as she could. She tilted her head backwards and smiled a small smile, indicating she was listening.

He began speaking in hushed tones, "My dearest child," he said, "Will you trust an old man, who loves you as much as his life itself, to tell you the truth about something that almost no one else knows, or cares to, for that matter?"

She had no idea what he was talking about, but as he sounded more serious than usual she turned slightly to see his face better. He looked into her eyes, and, as he continued to talk, he looked back outside the window where the skies were still being punctuated with bright flashes.

"Life has storms in it, Chelsea; lots of them—actually. And they're just part of being on this beautiful Earth of ours." He looked at her for a moment and then looked back outside; "But I want to let you in on a special secret about all storms, so that the next time you find yourself in the middle of one, feeling worried and afraid like you are now, you'll remember what your gramps told you and how it helped you to let go of the fear I know you're feeling. What do you think? Sound like something worth hearing?"

Chelsea turned further around in his lap to give him more attention, an indication she was willing to learn.

"You know your grandpa has been around for a long, long time, don't you, my child? Well, down through these many years I've been through storms of all possible shapes and sizes—big and small ones alike—and I can tell you one thing for an absolute certainty about every last one of them." He drew his eyes back from where they had been lost in the distance outside the window and, looking into Chelsea's eyes, finished his thought as simply but deliberately as he knew how:

"My child . . . I *never saw a storm that didn't pass.* "

He looked directly down at Chelsea to see if she had received the lesson he hoped to teach her. Could her young mind put two and two together? Would she realize he had told her the secret of how she could learn to live above any storm of turbulent thoughts and feelings? Evidently something of the lesson did get through to her because, in that same moment, she took a deep breath and he could feel her whole little body relax.

"Tell you what," he said, not wanting the impact of the lesson to be lost, "Let's just sit right where we are tonight and prove our little secret to ourselves. How does that sound to you? We'll wait right here in this chair, as long as it takes, and watch the storm until it disappears! Then, tomorrow morning, when we go for our horseback ride, I'll show you another secret about storms, something most folks never figure 'cause they're too busy looking the other way: Storms have a way of leaving the places they pass through refreshed and revitalized. Yep," he finished his last thought as they settled in for their storm watch, "A good storm makes everything new! So, what do you say? Do you think you're up for this kind of special adventure?"

From the bright look in her eyes he could see that Chelsea wasn't just "up" for this high adventure; she was wide awake and ready for her first lesson in learning how to watch storms disappear!

There are three key lessons we should take from this story. First, before we can learn to free ourselves from our own fearful reactions to unwanted events, we must realize just how worthless fear actually is—especially when we turn to it to protect us from what are essentially bad dreams wrought from the darkened works of our own imagination! When it comes to these stormy moments in life, what we resist always persists. In truth, it is our *not wanting* to be in a psychological storm that produces the very storm of unwanted feelings that we don't want!

One of the things that makes uncertain times so hard to bear is the flood of fearful feelings that seems to travel with them, like hard rains we are sure will soon fall from a distant, dark cloud on the horizon. But such fear is neither a natural nor necessary part of uncertainty, and this you can prove to yourself if you're willing to be a conscious storm watcher.

What does it mean to be a storm watcher? Whenever conditions occur that look like they are front-runners of a storm of some kind, choose in that same moment to sit back and become quietly aware of yourself. Watch how the newly formed, agitated thoughts and feelings within you want to drag you into dark imaginings in order to produce the storm clouds of some scary "maybe." Each time you can awaken yourself from this self-produced nightmare and pull the curtains closed on its performance, you will reclaim your natural confidence and calm. Now let's gather these last two lessons together for the third and main point of this study section.

Just as the eye of a hurricane doesn't exist without the great winds that circle it, neither does that dark or troubled sense of "I" exist as the temporary center of our struggling self without all of the negative thoughts whirling around it. We already know that the conditions that produce physical storms always pass naturally, and that when they are gone, so too is the storm they produced. Now it's time for us to learn that the same holds true for any of the psychological storms that shake us. Not only can we discover the secret of how to let any of these inner storms pass through us without fearing them, but also if we will do our part in waking up to, and letting go of, the unconscious conditions within us that create these storms, then we have learned the secret of how to end any storm before it begins!

ASK THE MASTERS

QUESTION: I love the idea of living in a world without storms, but given how much turmoil and trouble there seems to be everywhere, including in ourselves, where do we find such an elevated state of self?

ANSWER: *Peace of mind produces right values, right values produce right thoughts. Right thoughts produce right actions, and right actions produce work which will be a material reflection for others to see of the serenity at the center of it all.*
—Robert M. Pirsig

QUESTION: Why do so many wisdom teachings stress the idea of inner work to cultivate self-watchfulness? I want to be free of my fears, but to tell you the truth, the whole idea of seeing myself as I am scares me. Is there no other way?

ANSWER: *The shell must be cracked apart if what is in it is to come out, for if you want the kernel you must break the shell. And therefore if you want to discover nature's nakedness you must destroy its symbols, and the farther you get in the nearer you come to its essence. When you come to the One that gathers all things up into itself, there you must stay.*
—Meister Eckhart

KEY LESSONS IN REVIEW

1. When we are awakened at night from a nightmare, we realize with a start that we had been sleeping; but when a dark state overcomes us in the daylight hours, we believe we are awake, never suspecting that our bad dream unfolds as it does because we remain asleep within ourselves.

2. While the desire to be perfect runs through the very fiber of our soul, how to fulfill the longing of this greater love is a question few find the answer to, and here is why: The path to self-perfection weaves its secret way through the land of imperfection, where only the conscious awareness of where we actually are changes forever where we stand.

3. Never agree that you are powerless in the face of dark and unwanted moments, because instead of mindlessly aching, you can always reclaim your attention and remember this truth: The Light of God is greater than any shadows that come over you, so instead of hating the darkness, look for this light and watch how your life grows brighter.

4. It isn't until we realize that our True Nature can never be known, only continually discovered, that we become the conscious and fearless explorers of reality that we are created to be—moving in and out of complementary or conflicting moments alike with the same ease as a dolphin delightfully carving its way through the endless currents of the sea.

5. Whenever we can remember the truth that all dark thoughts and feelings require our consent to punish us, and that these negative states are, in themselves, literally nothing without the powers we grant them, then we become the conqueror of what would have overcome us!

CHAPTER SIX

The Power
to Dismiss Discontentment
From Your Life

I t is no stretch of the imagination to say that many days most
people wrestle with some form of discontentment in life. Now, if
we add to this disgruntled condition an equal, if not greater,
amount of time spent searching for solutions to "cure" this conflic-
tion, we arrive at a surprising discovery: a great deal of our time on
earth is spent trying to dodge feelings of being discontented! We're
about to discover how needless it is for any of us to live with this
kind of negativity, a process that begins with making a short list of
those suspects commonly seen as being our comfort stealers.
Personal studies like these are invaluable because the first step in
learning to let go of what disturbs us is to increase our awareness of
how its root dynamic works within us. Wisdom teachings confirm
this truth. Only the light of conscious awareness can effectively change
the unconscious cause of these unwanted patterns.

Here's a surprising insight to keep in mind during the investigation that follows: The usual sorts of discontentment that darken our days, those unwelcome visitors that trouble the mind and sour the heart, behave much like a bunch of bees lined up in a row to enter their hive. They can only enter one at a time. This special knowledge—that discontented thoughts and feelings are themselves limited in the way they can enter into our psychic system—will prove very helpful to us later on as we learn how to separate ourselves from their stinging states.

Depending on how the day breaks for us, we may experience any or all of the following discontented conditions. This list is presented in no particular order; it is intended only to illustrate the opening point of this study, that is, that most of us spend a lot more time trying to deal with discontentment than is obvious at first glance. As always, for extra spiritual benefit you might want to make your own list of those vitality-stealing thoughts and feelings you suspect are active in you.

We often find ourselves feeling discontent about our life whenever we:

1. Compare our present level of health and energy to those better days when we felt a stronger wind at our back

2. Start thinking about our inescapable responsibility to provide for ourselves or significant others

3. Take a close look at our physical appearance and find we are not buff enough

4. Review our relationships with family or friends and remember how these people rarely treat us as we think they should

5. Run headlong into self-compromising behaviors beyond our seeming strength or ability to change

6. Take that almost daily inventory of our personal possessions or lack of them

7. Find ourselves unable to change or otherwise control someone near to us

8. Start reliving our uneventful past, or imagine an equally unpromising future

9. Measure ourselves against others and, through comparison, conclude that they have more reason to be content than we do

The sole purpose of this list is to help us recognize how much grief we have come to take for granted, as though being perpetually negative is somehow natural. This insight brings us to another important and somewhat startling discovery: Discontentment always makes perfect sense to the discontented!

By the light of our impersonal study we can see two bright new truths: much of our time is spent identifying the so-called cause of our discontented condition, and the rest of our time is taken up trying to change our unwanted situation into what we imagine will better suit our pleasure. Of course this description puts a kind of positive spin on what amounts to one's never-ending whirl of wishes, but the facts are that these dreams of a better time to come do not originate with our True Self. They are the incessant creation of one's unconscious thought nature, that ever-seeking, never-quite-satisfied self whose endless aspirations we all know too well!

This level of self knows only the kind of comfort that it can imagine into being. For instance, who among us hasn't found themselves conjuring up some imagined pleasure when faced with the pain of some contradiction in life that seems greater than our ability to deal with? And this imagined contentment is fine, *if* we believe an imaginary umbrella has the power to keep us dry in a downpour! To become conscious of this unconscious dynamic effectively cancels its authority over us. We don't have to live from any such self that is always seeking to exchange what we are in the moment for its more idealized conception of what it imagines can complete us. Key to this finding is that this would-be contented nature is inseparable from the discontentment that it breeds as it drags us through its comparison of what is to what should be.

Here's something even more surprising about this level of our discontented self: this nature is not just driven along by its unhappiness but, in fact, has no independent existence apart from it. It requires that something always be wrong in order for it to set things right. In other words, the contentment this self seeks only exists as long as its sense of being discontented is allowed to remain. The life span of this discontented nature is the length of time it takes to hand you over to its opposite: the projected pleasure that awaits you when you arrive at your imagined destination. But, as we know to be true, we no sooner arrive at this chosen port of pleasure than we become aware again of what is not right with where we now are. You can see now how the cycle of discontentment starts all over again!

Awakening to see this cycle of discontent for what it is not only empowers us to cancel it, but it also brings to an end the strain of living under the unseen contradiction in our consciousness: the hope that one's discontentment can be resolved by the very nature that creates and sustains it. Clearly a whole new order of solution is required. Finding this solution begins with a simple question that summarizes what we have been learning so far: Who in his or her right mind believes—even for a moment—that the path to lasting contentment would be paved by continually thinking about everything that is seen as missing from one's life? Such a path may promise pleasure to come but, as we are uncovering here, its steps are spiked with discontentment.

We have been the unwitting servants of a thought nature whose appetite is unappeasable. Its life is fueled by opposites that cannot cancel each other, any more than picking up a sword can kill the fear in us that creates those whom we detest. The clearer our under-standing of our present condition becomes, the more certain and surgical become our daily actions. We can end our agreement to live with this unenlightened nature. Now let's look at what we must do to free ourselves from our discontentment and the divided nature that sits at its core.

First, we must be willing to see the futility of our struggle to acquire more of those things in life that have already proven them-selves powerless to please us. In concert with this effort comes the inner work of deliberately detaching ourselves from the familiar sense of self that promises us comfort even as it continues to sow the seeds of our discontent.

In spite of how daunting such an effort may seem at first, we can succeed with our wish to let go because we are beginning to act from the power that our own awakening grants us. Nothing is greater; no force can frustrate such a light as it dawns within. Here is why this holds true: We are starting to see through the source of discontent-ment. We now understand how the thought-self habitually perceives what its conditioned natures sees as not right about our lives, and then compares this negative image to what it further imagines ought to be taking place. And presto, we are in pain of some sort! These are the opposites at work within us. This is what has been working on us, dragging us into ever-deeper stages of discontentment with life.

But we can declare, "Enough is enough." The divided nature that embodies these opposites is not our True Self; it is but a shadow, a single aspect of our own original contented character. We can learn to call upon a new I within that understands the futility of continu-ing to vest ourselves in the "hope of things seen." Rather than giving

ourselves over to these malcontent feelings with their empty promises of a better tomorrow, we can let them go instead and gain possession of ourselves in the Now.

This brings us to these last important notes: Our new intention
to consciously detach ourselves from this discontented nature and
the objects of its life is not an act of denial or resistance to whatever
we may be feeling in the moment. This shift in the sense of "I" is a
deliberate *re-placement* of our attention. Instead of trying to escape
this discontented sense of self, we bring it—along with its troubles
and plans for freedom—into the new and higher awareness of our
True Nature. By daring to bring what would displease us about our
life into the light of our new self-understanding, that light itself sees
to it that we emerge victorious.

Perhaps you might be wondering: Why on earth do we have to
deal with such seemingly complicated concerns? As shocking or challenging as this next idea may be, for now, please consider its truth.
Before we are through we will prove the fact of it beyond doubt.

The Divine—that great, intelligent, and compassionate Creator
whose singular life sits behind the expression of all things—whatever name one attributes to this eternal Light, it *itself* created this
seemingly unanswerable discontentment in us.

Why would Goodness itself give us such a mysterious gift, one
that is so hard to grasp? Because it is only through our trials with
being discontented that we can come to see that there is only one
true course for us to take. The signs point unmistakably. Experience
confirms what we are just beginning to consider. There is but one
source of perfect contentment: to realize our life within that unend-
ing Life by whose compassionate light we can see all that we are,
and all that we are not, in the Now.

The knowledge you need to start letting go of this discontented
self is in your hands. Use these truths to help take yourself beyond

that unhappiness that comes with living from a nature that only knows about an imagined contentment to come. Start right now by *knowing* that the contentment your heart longs for already dwells in you and only waits for you to prepare a place for it by your remembrance of its peace.

THE SPIRITUAL SECRET THAT ALLOWS YOU TO DEFEAT ANY DISCOURAGEMENT

As we all know, there are trying times when states of discouragement literally dog us—following us around as if they're waiting for us to fall down, never to rise again. On these days, our own lackluster emotions are hounded by thoughts barking at us that nothing is right with our lives. Sound familiar? On these same days, even our smallest wish to part ways with these painful states gets pushed under by waves of doubt so that our resolve to not sink into a malaise feels like a futile struggle against the inevitable!

When falling into deeper and deeper states of feeling discouraged, we can almost hear these unspoken words within, "What's the point? Why bother?" Then, as though we have heard from the Fates themselves, we accept the dreariness of some *can't do* negative state as our guide. Is this how it must be? Must we identify ourselves with what discourages us? The answer to these questions is decidedly *no*! But to free ourselves from the spell that discouragement casts over our consciousness requires that we uncover the ways that this negative state steals our will and turns us into will-less toadstools! So, let's begin our journey with a great truth: All discouraging feelings are a lie.

Now perhaps you are already wondering how something with the power to wreck a human life can be unreal. Please make the mental note that this initial truth doesn't mean that we don't feel the weight of bleak moments; and neither does it mean that many of us don't fall beneath their spell and become trampled under their powerful illusion.

No, discouraging states of self can land upon us with the force of a thousand regrets. They sneak in and steal our vitality, infusing the very atmosphere around us with misgivings about our very lives. Clearly, just contending with such an adversary is a task, let alone overcoming its negative influences and coming out on top. But that is exactly what we are going to do, beginning with this surprising insight: it makes no difference why we feel the presence of some discouraging darkness within us. When it comes to our eventual conquest of our feelings of discouragement them, the actual cause of them is of no consequence. Let me explain this revelation.

Sometimes we feel discouraged because our past efforts to meaningfully change our lives have not prevailed over what challenges us. We think, why bother to try now? Perhaps we are disheartened because one of our main hopes for happiness suddenly proves hopeless. Maybe we get downcast some days because our body, or our mind, is no longer capable of doing what it once could in our younger years and all we see on the horizon are more limitations.

When it comes to these dispiriting states, the point is it makes no difference what they would have us believe is to blame for their bitterness. The truth is that these dark states don't need to find a reason outside of us to wreck us. They draw upon all the cause they need to exist within us from the content of our own past experience! What does this mean?

Negative states, all dark energies that enervate us, only succeed at draining us because they are capable of making us see mentally and emotionally charged images of past defeats. These images, drawn from the storehouse of our memories, seem so real that they validate the existence of our negative conclusions, which brings us to a key lesson deserving of our special attention.

The only power dark, discouraging states hold over us is that they get us to identify with feelings of being powerless. And when such strong feelings of futility are accompanied by what is seen, in our own mind's eye, as being valid because we are given over to unconsciously recall the considerations that make them so, then boom! The trap is sprung. We become the unwitting captives of our own negative imagination! Had enough of feeling like you are never enough? Good! Let the following truths do their healing work.

When we feel discouraged it is just that: we are without the courage we need to attempt whatever it is before us. Feeling emotionally drained and mentally depleted, we seem to have nothing to call upon to overcome life's challenges. We never feel so alone as when we are in the company of dark, discouraging thoughts and feelings, but this dreaded sense of isolation is actually a secret part of its punishing plan. All such hopeless thoughts and feelings *want* us to feel alone.

Here is a quick glimpse of an amazing insight to help us defeat this darkness at work within us: discouraged states of self can only breed themselves in a specialized sense of isolation, in a dark medium that is able to effect in us the illusion that we have been cut off from the endless resources of Real Life. In other words, the reason why discouraging states hold us captive as they do is that they convince us that the limited darkness of their reality is all there is for us to live within! But such small states only have this last word about the world we live in as long as we agree with what they tell us is true about our possibilities. We can do better than consent to live like this, and here are the steps that ensure our freedom:

First, we must know in our hearts that our True Nature is not created to live as a captive of any dark condition. If you have never heard this before, then hear it now: no power on earth can restrain the soul that seeks its liberation in the uncontainable truth.

Next we realize, to whatever depth we can conceive, that our own awareness is a living and intelligent feature of the ever-present

Now within which it dwells—and that this same timeless Now is omnipresent. It dwells everywhere already, knowing no boundaries. And here we catch a glimpse of another timeless truth: nothing in the universe can capture our awareness any more than a cloud has the power to envelop the sky.

What these last few discoveries teach us is that our awareness of discouragement, or any negative state for that matter, transcends its boundary and already dwells beyond the limits of its confining darkness. This brings us to this discouragement-busting truth: whenever we will lend our attention to the inner task of working to transcend some dark state at work within us, then in that same moment, even if we don't see the immediate fruits of our effort, we will have already begun to release ourselves from its restrictions. For our effort to be conscious of our condition instead of remaining its captive, fresh energies flood over and through us, lifting us into the new understanding that who we really are can never be held back! Our willingness to bring that dark, discouraged state into our awareness of it, instead of allowing it to define what we are aware of, has changed our very relationship with life!

Now the upward path ahead, which was closed off to us only a moment before, opens wide its narrow gate as we open ourselves to the endless resources of a Living Truth. The Now nature newly active within us cannot be walled in by anything, which means that the limitations of former restrictions no longer exist for us. The darkness that once dominated us is literally dismissed because we have chosen the Living Light itself to be our advocate.

So now we know: the Way is already made for us to live in perfect contentment; we need never again suffer for no reason. More than this, we may take great comfort in knowing that nothing in the universe can stop us from realizing this victorious order of our own being, because the Divine has already seen to the truth of it. We need only agree to pay the cost of this higher consciousness, and we will find that the coins we need are already right there in our pocket.

CANCEL THE TEN CAUSES OF NEEDLESS HEARTACHES

Why do we accept so much unhappiness in our lives today? If you think this supposition is untrue, ask yourself why people spend so much time seeking ways to distract themselves with empty pleasures? Or why so many people push themselves along one spiritual path after another, blindly hoping that *something* will happen to mitigate their sense of emptiness? To understand such questions we must be willing to explore a few of the broader questions concerning what seems like an epidemic of human suffering. And please remember this spiritual axiom as we proceed: Anything in us that resists exploring the cause of a sorrow is itself part of the pain that prefers to stay unexposed.

Keeping these ideas in mind, consider this: is the kind of pain most people tolerate really necessary? And if, as many would presume, these various heartaches, fears, and frustrations are part and parcel of participating in life, can we be so sure that these same pains are an inescapable attribute of reality? Or are these dark moments unnecessary, just shadows of our misunderstanding about what is possible in life and what is not?

Now I realize that in today's highly spiritualized slick atmosphere, the suggestion that some things in life are impossible may not find favor. After all, according to the reasoning of many of today's so-called masters and gurus, nothing is impossible for those realized beings illuminated by the "light" of their exclusive teachings, sentiments easily swallowed by the weak and weary.

But there are things in this life that cannot be done. And, as we are about to discover, it is our repeated attempts to do these things that actually produce much, if not all, of our everyday unhappiness—

an unhappiness that we erroneously blame upon other people and circumstances in life. The brief explanation that follows reveals both the truth of this and why we need to see it.

We begin with the fact that each of us does have the power, in one way or another, to do as we wish when we wish it. The issue at hand isn't that we can't do what we wish, but that these actions cannot deliver the result intended by our original wish.

For instance, take a person who wants to win everyone's approval. He believes that it is possible to adjust his behavior so that whomever he meets will like him. This is his wish, and to make it come true, he changes his behavior with everyone he encounters, known to him or not. We can agree that it *is* possible for him to act out his hope of being loved by all he meets.

But what is impossible for him to do—regardless of how any particular encounter turns out—is to free himself of his nagging insecurity by acting out what this fearful nature compels him to do. And since we also know that it is this same strained sense of himself—of feeling inept or insufficient—that drives him to seek its opposite, for example, trying to impress people to win their approval, then what is it at work in him? What is it that is *actually* interfacing with these people he wants to win over? It is his own undetected weakness, a fact hidden from him because of his identification with his pretend powers of self-command!

Now add to this last idea the fact that others can easily see this weakness at work within us. We may not be conscious of our own psychological shortcomings, but we can sure recognize them in others! And more, it is the nature of all such unconscious weakness to judge and then pounce upon anyone else displaying it. Put these facts together and it becomes obvious that not only is it impossible for this one person to fulfill his wish, but *his attempt to do so is causing the very suffering he so resists.*

Here is the heart of this lesson, the specific points of which I will make clearer in a special exercise: No *opposite can cancel itself*. It is impossible. We can draw upon the following short metaphor to help us better understand this crucial spiritual truth.

Imagine a sad pencil that wants all the pens of the world to acknowledge the strength of its carbon center, but it can't win its way! So, it decides not to be a pencil any more. And while one end of this pained pencil concocts ways to change itself into something that is no longer a lead-filled wooden stick, in the end—by the very need it has to dream such dreams to escape itself—it remains pained for remaining a "mere" pencil.

The more we learn about the unnecessary suffering these unseen opposites create in us through our unconscious relationship with them, the freer we become from unconscious drives to attempt the impossible. For example, it is impossible to bring an end to emotional suffering by imagining a new joy. Can you see from our study why this is true?

The self that is moved to do this kind of imagining does not understand that some unseen force of sorrow or distress fuels its dream engine. As a consequence, the more it works to imagine some hoped-for happiness, the more identified it becomes with the opposite of what is driving this dream of brighter times to come.

Our lives are meant to be bright, noble, and ever ascending. This promise of our true potential is made good in us by fulfilling our possibilities and not through the interminable struggle of trying to prove what is impossible. Most of our sorrows are the stressful offspring of trying to be something we have no *real* need to be; they are born for attempting to do what cannot—and need not—be done.

The following Ten Causes of Needless Heartaches reveal how we cause ourselves unnecessary suffering. Please keep in mind that each of these ten insights contains two key ideas: First, whenever we are goaded into attempting the "impossible," we not only suffer defeat, but we also strengthen the self that would have us believe it's possible to put a fire out with gasoline. Second, as we awaken to see these false workings in our mind, we also see there is only one possible solution to end the suffering they cause: we must stop listening to and obeying their foolish advice. In other words, as soon as we see that the healing we hope for *begins* with releasing our unseen relationship with the parts of ourselves that are responsible for our self-hurting, the sooner our heartaches end.

Now, let's look at ten small places in our lives where we are trying to do the impossible and where, as a result of our misunderstanding, we are still sowing and reaping the harvest of frustration and heartache.

1. It is impossible *to make* others see where they have made a mistake.

2. It is impossible to be carried to a secure and peaceful harbor on a ship crafted by anxiety or fueled by fearful feelings.

3. It is impossible to gain real happiness at the expense of someone else's pain.

4. It is impossible to genuinely elevate yourself by pushing another person lower.

5. It is impossible to take advantage of others without living in secret fear of them.

6. It is impossible to realize the fulfillment of the Divine as long as we remain filled with ourselves.

7. It is impossible to rise above any fear or worry whose root we have not found, uncovered, and removed from our own present misunderstanding.

8. It is impossible to receive forgiveness in life without having learned what it means to freely forgive.

9. It is impossible to wish another person any kind of ill, for any reason, and not be made sick ourselves.

10. It is impossible to resist or hate any condition in life and learn from it at the same time.

See how many ways you can enlarge this list through insights of your own about the ways in which you are being tricked into punishing yourself. This is priceless self-study and it rewards the sincere seeker with a life free of unnecessary sorrow. Remember and honor your intention to win Real Life by daring to act out the truths that set you free. This is the challenge, and the cost, of earning true contentment in life.

YOUR NEW AUTHORITY OVER WHATEVER HURTS YOU

We have reached an important point in our study concerning the dismissal of those dark states that steal happiness. Wishing to be free, without taking action toward our intention, is meaningless; we must employ the truths we uncover, or we will never realize the possibility of their true power, which is to help us walk away from what has been wrecking us. But with this new understanding in mind we must also realize that the truth that sets us free is not for hire; it does not so much "work" for us as it is our silent *partner*, producing the new life we long for. This means several things.

First, as we have been learning, we must be receptive to truth's instruction in the Now; only conscious awareness of our aching can lead us to what authentically answers it, ending it. But secondly we must, ourselves, be true in the same moment to what we know is the truth of that moment. For instance, speaking of discontentment, once we see that giving our consent to relive any regret is nothing but walking into a dark cave—cleverly concealed by a sign that reads: "Enter here to escape your past,"—then we no longer stand before this tunnel of thoughts wondering if this time reliving a torment will give us a new result! It won't; it hasn't; it can't, and somewhere from within us we know this to be true. So now we must *do* the truth we know. We must refuse, no matter what the seeming cost in the moment, to take part in any conversation with those parts of us that have proven themselves, time and time again, to compromise us. The following short story points us in the right direction of how we can begin to put our new knowledge into practice.

Tessa was a little nervous walking up to the large, double-hung carved-glass doors, but she took a deep breath and stepped up to push against the weight she imagined they would have. To her surprise, just before her hands made contact, they started to slowly open by themselves—leaving her standing there in the doorway, arms extended like she was sleepwalking. A compulsory glance at the people seated ahead of her in the dining area confirmed a few had caught her in this unsophisticated act so, to recover from this, she feigned as though she was stretching out her arms, even yawning a bit as if she was bored with the scene she was entering. The truth was a different story: She was almost tingling with excitement!

For one thing, she had not seen her older sister, Claudia, in nearly six months; it was hard to believe that much time had flown by. But now none of that mattered anymore. She was in Hollywood, visiting her favorite sister who had been hired by a major motion picture studio as the stand-in for one of the most popular actresses in the business. And if that wasn't enough, here she was in the Commissary of the Stars, the studio's private restaurant. Not only was she going to see some genuine stars of the big screen, but she was also going to actually dine in the same room with them while she and her sister shared a lunch. So rapt in these thoughts was she that Tessa didn't know she was lost in a daydream until the maitre d' startled her.

"My goodness," he said, smiling, "but you *do* look like your sister. Claudia told me I would easily recognize you, but who would have thought!" Continuing without a breath he went on: "Your sister is going to be a few minutes late. She phoned only a few moments ago to ask that I look for you, and voila! Here you are! Let me show you to your table."

Without waiting for her to respond he began walking toward a corner table in the rear of the room surrounded on all sides by mirrors. And even though he wasn't looking at her, he continued speaking. "My name is Roberto, and it is my great pleasure to meet you. Follow me, please."

Tessa did what felt like a quick march step to catch up to him, and when she at last slid into her chair she not only felt the weight come off her feet, but with this fell away the burden of an immense sense of being a fish out of water. She took in a deep gulp of air, let it out quietly, and began looking around the room for the first time.

The place was elegant. People in leather booths were speaking in hushed tones and her ears strained to catch the secrets she just knew would be tomorrow's entertainment headlines. In fact, so drawn was she into her imagined drama of the place, filling in the sordid details of the private conversations she couldn't quite overhear, that she never noticed a sudden shift in the atmosphere of the room. The whole place had fallen into an almost palpable quiet, something like the stillness that comes over a jungle floor whenever a top predator is on the prowl. Her senses came on alert. But it was too late.

By the time she turned back around in her seat to face the front of the dining room, she found herself looking directly into the piercing eyes of a small, elegantly dressed olive-skinned man standing right in front of her table. Instantly, instinctively, she knew that he was the reason for the silence in the room. Equally as fast, she wondered why he was perched over her table like a falcon on a tree-top. Then she recognized him, and with this her heart fell straight to the bottom of her stomach.

It was Simon Manleshart, the world famous director of the very film her sister had come to Hollywood to work on. She took in a stiff, short breath; so many conflicting images raced through her mind all at once, she hardly knew whether to stand up and warmly greet him or make a break for the front door! But all she could do was sit there, her mind reviewing the letters that Claudia had sent her—one awful story after another about this man's legendary temper and arrogance. She felt a strange impression pass through her when, a second later, she realized that she was still staring into his eyes. She thought to herself, "This must be something like how a bird feels, hypnotized by a snake just before it strikes." Little did Tessa know the precision of her intuition—for that's exactly what happened next: Simon launched into a viperous verbal attack.

"*Who* do you think you are," he literally bellowed at her, "to make *me* come looking for you?" Tessa felt her eyes fly wide open in disbelief, but every other part of her was frozen. Her involuntary silence seemed to further enrage him, but she couldn't find her voice.

"Really?" he said sarcastically, as if she had said something. "So you don't care that we are on a tight filming schedule, and that it's *my* neck on the line?" And then, looking around the room without moving his head, assured he had captured everyone's attention, he kept going.

"Let me tell you something, you stupid little girl," his face grew more red than it had been moments before, "that's what's wrong with everyone like you: All you care about is yourselves! Now, get up," he barked at her, "and get back to the set where you belong!"

Not a muscle had moved in Tessa's face, and though she felt utterly helpless in her humiliation, she knew she had to respond.

Then he gave her the jolt she needed.

"What *are* you, an idiot?" he yelled through a sneer that his mouth seemed stuck in. "Now you get up and do what I say or you will never work in this business again. Do I make myself clear?"

So stunned by this assault was she that Tessa felt something like she did when she accidentally shocked herself silly with a bad extension cord. And as her mind began to find its way back to sensibility, the urge to answer his accusations—to just appease him so he would go away—was almost overwhelming. But even as her mind raced to find face-saving excuses and explanations, Tessa could sense something else trying to get her attention; a completely different idea was taking shape in her heart, an answer she intuitively knew was the right one for the moment—if only she could stem the tide of fear long enough for it to form itself in her. And then, just like that, she knew exactly how to handle his angry and cruel-hearted accusations.

Tessa sat up straight in her chair, lifting her chin at the same time; and though no one could see it, she smiled to herself. Then, for the first time since this embarrassment had begun, she deliberately returned the director's gaze—meeting his eyes with an unexpected strength that made him look away. And when—centered as she now felt herself to be in the seat of a powerful new understanding—she found her voice to answer his attack. He was far more surprised by the words she spoke than she was for finding the courage to speak them:

"You have obviously mistaken me for someone over whom you must have considerable power, but you have just tried to bully the wrong woman." And then, with a delicious finality she said:

"*I don't answer to you!*"

And with that Tessa took her attention back, turned slightly in her seat to return the smile of a person across the room who was smiling approvingly at her and, by her actions, effectively told Mr. Manleshart that he had been dismissed.

As the color drained from his face he started to sputter a broken phrase or two, but with no audience left to either intimidate or entertain, he did the only thing left for him to do. He spun on his heels and walked out of the dining room, leaving Tessa in peace.

If you want to know how to answer any ache you feel, here's the *real* answer: We need never answer *any* part of ourselves that wants to punish us, intimidate, or otherwise drag us down. Our power to dismiss these tormenting thoughts and feelings comes to us in proportion to our awakening understanding that we do not work for them. Therefore, we owe them nothing—not one consideration, not even the wish that they would leave us alone!

We can discover the same liberating truth that Tessa did. Our refusal to answer to these dark, discouraging, self-wrecking states leaves them with no one to try to push around. And without someone to bully about or otherwise drag down into their conflicted world, *they have no world to rule over*! Our awakened consciousness reclaims our right to be self-ruling because *its* power knocks all would-be dictators from their throne.

ASK THE MASTERS

QUESTION: I have a friend who says he would make more of an effort to drop his defeated attitudes toward the possibility of a new life, but he's convinced there's so much wrong with him that he doesn't have a chance to succeed.

ANSWER: *Being overly concerned with your faults is worse for your spiritual condition than the fault itself.*

—Jeanne Guyon

QUESTION: What's the singular most important step for me to take on this path if I want to learn how to let go of my constant sense of discontentment with my life?

ANSWER: *We could come into a new reality of our being and perceive everything in a new relation if we can stand still from self-thinking and self-willing and stop the wheel of imagination and the senses.*

—Jacob Boehme

KEY LESSONS IN REVIEW

1. As long as we willingly jump on board that dark train of thoughts and feelings called our discontentment, desperately trying to reach the end of the line where we hope happiness awaits us, we will never discover that all such discontentment is a lie and that its desire to find fulfillment outside of our own heart is a part of that lie.

2. Just as a swarm of flies that darkens the sky is swept aside by a single breeze, so too can the pervasive negative states that darken one's heart and mind be brushed away—if we will only dare to come awake to ourselves and ask that tormenting spirit a single question: Upon what is your authority based?

3. Those parts of us that whisper from some unseen corner of our heart, that tell us our effort to know the truth of ourselves is useless, are nothing but the dark voices of uselessness itself. These negative states must try to denigrate our fledgling hope for the higher life because if they can't succeed in darkening our heart to make it inhabitable for them, then they and their forces of despair will have nowhere else to dwell!

4. The only true solution to that constant press of discontentment in our lives is not to acquire more of what has proven powerless

to please us, but to consciously detach ourselves from that level of self that believes the path to contentment is paved by continually thinking about what is missing from one's life.

5. Just as any light brought to bear upon some dark place breaks that darkness down until it must disappear, so is it true that our effort and struggle to be conscious in a moment of being negative gives us the inner light we need to negate and finally dismiss these dark unconscious forces.

CHAPTER SEVEN

Use Eternal Principles to Empower Yourself in the Now

The more we can learn to quietly observe ourselves and others, the more we see how much we all share one kind of behavior: moment to moment we are all in search of a little peace, a measure of happiness we can call our own. Here's a man seated at his desk dreaming of when he will have his life to himself; over there is a woman at the luncheon counter trying to resolve some relationship issue in her mind. And so it goes: everyone everywhere is looking to find his or her slice of heaven. Some seek their heaven in worldly things—within plans for a better tomorrow filled with new pleasures. For others bliss means having someone to hold, or maybe being held rapt by some natural wonder. And some are sure that their culturally conditioned belief in some heaven-to-come is the same as living in the peace of its ever-present light.

But, regardless of where one seeks his or her heaven in *this* world, two things ought to be clear: first, our *imagined* heavens never last; they lose their luster. Reasons abound for why the glory of these treasures fade, but in the end it's the same story: one way or another reality collides with our dreamboat, and as it sinks into life's unknown waters so too does our hope that *this time* our ship had come in!

Secondly, it isn't until we have had enough of coming up empty that it occurs to us that not only have we been looking for heaven in all the wrong places, but maybe, just maybe, what our heart longs for isn't to be found where we have been searching for it. Our intuition serves us true: upon the silent halls and walls of true spiritual sanctuaries world-over is invisibly etched the words, "Why seek ye the permanent in the passing, the eternal in the temporary?"

I live on top of a small mountain in southern Oregon where each morning, from a chair seated next to a large window in my small house, I have the good fortune to sit quietly and watch the world turn. Right outside, usually less than ten to twelve feet away from where I am seated, it is as though Mother Nature mounts a wildlife parade just for me. Deer, wild turkey, gray tree squirrels, rabbits, and more than a dozen species of birds all congregate and then move through an area just beneath a cluster of spreading oak trees. The birds come for the seed I provide in a number of stations, and the turkeys come for their table scraps. Why the rest appear as they do is anyone's guess. Maybe they just enjoy the party!

At any rate, come early March, signs of spring appear and this change means many things to my visiting friends. For most birds, mating season begins in earnest. This usually means lots of singing, posturing, and aggressive, territorial behavior. For some of the other creatures, this time heralds a season for giving birth to young conceived some months before.

But regardless of these varying conditions, one thing remains common to one and all—and it is apparent to anyone watching with an eye willing to observe and learn: these creatures are constantly active. They are as alert and as responsive to life going on around them as is a silk spiderweb to the slightest summer's breeze.

Along with this natural feature of all wild creatures, in fact very much at the root of what enables them to expend so much vital energy, is another highly noticeable behavior: their lives are spent in a never-ending search for food. Apart from propagating their own species, feeding themselves is their principal work on this earth. Which brings us to this point:

The silent turning of the seasons, the latent desire of all creatures to fulfill the purpose for their being, the invisible hand that ensures that necessary supplies of foodstuffs will be there for them at the right moment—these elements, their balance and concert with one another, all speak of what the Wise have called the "Invisible Eternals."

These Invisible Eternals are the unseen timeless principles that sit behind the manifestation of our physical world, and are to its existence what the sun is to the shadows that pay silent witness to the radiance of their Creator. To be able to see these eternal forces as the true backdrop of a greater reality is to become a witness to an intelligent universe at work in an ever-present Now.

When one becomes consciously aware of these Invisible Eternals, one discovers and enters into a whole new order of reality—where intelligence, action, and harmony are as one thing. Herein the Light shines upon and animates all creatures alike, and even conflict serves something greater than its lesser causes.

This journey of awareness between one's first glimpse of a higher reality, and the realization of this as the ground of one's own being, *is* the spiritual path. It is the task required of all those who would enter these higher worlds within themselves. And we are intended to know this interior heaven while we dwell here on earth. Make no mistake about this.

Peel away the accumulated coatings of all the socially accept-able translations of the great religious scriptures, and at their golden root we find one basic and bright premise: the *here and now* heaven for which our heart longs, just as a river reaches out for the sea, runs *through us* Now. The great Christian mystic, Boehme, points out that Christ taught this same truth, "My sheep hear my voice, and I know them, and they follow me, and I give them the eternal life." Here, Christ did not say, "You may know life eternal in a time to come," i.e., after death, but rather *here* and *now*, in this life.

If we have the eyes to see these Invisible Eternals, where the celestial is hidden in the common, and the ears to hear how their timeless reality corresponds to the workings of our own conscious-ness, then we stand prepared to do the inner work it takes to realize our own True Nature.

SOW THE SEEDS OF A HIGHER AND HAPPIER LIFE

What is the nature of true inner work, the kind that permanently trans-forms our being, and how can we be sure it is required of us? When is this work to be done, and who, or what, determines all of the above? These are the questions that sincere seekers have asked since time began. For now, one thing ought to be clear: to enter the true Now, where a timeless intelligence awaits, awake within itself, requires first that we align ourselves with the eternal principles that are its secret foundation.

Our need to discover and realize these Invisible Eternals cannot be overstated because the truth is we are their embodiment. This fact makes it possible for us to awaken to their existence, align our-selves with their will, and realize our oneness with them. Now let's take one of these great principles and explore its wisdom in order to increase our own. The "proof" of the following insight is self-evident: Throughout creation all lesser things have their origin within some-thing greater. For instance, the branch owes its being to the vine from which it originates; the rivers run back to the seas that give them birth. And so it is with the Invisible Eternals. Among as well as within them are found *greater* and *lesser* truths.

With these insights to guide us, let's look into one of the most fundamental of these principles taught by every great teacher: We reap what we sow. In these so-called progressive times, this all but forgotten principle is as simple as it is prophetic. Share this simple fact with someone who hates his life, and he will hate you for the truth you tell about why he feels as he does!

Everywhere we look, people are concerned with essentially one thing: getting what they want, when they want it, and as fast as possible. The fires that fuel their appetite for this envisioned success create so much smoke that they lose sight of the fact that all they reap for their insistent sowing are the cold ashes of regret raked out of broken relationships.

If we are ever to realize the integrity and consistent kindness of our True Nature, if we long to know something of heaven while we live on earth, then we must sow the seeds that bring that higher life into fruition. One cannot expect to reap what one does not sow; and merely hoping for a higher life is not sowing true spiritual seeds, any more than climbing an imagined mountain is the same as reaching its top.

To sow spiritual seeds means that we do spiritual work. Spiritual work is always interior work first, even if, as a matter of course, this work becomes manifest through exterior action. What is this interior work by which we sow the seeds of the celestial within us? Following are four ways to sow the seeds of a higher and happier life.

1. We must work to not burden others or ourselves with past regrets, disappointments, or fearful future visions, even as we learn to ask truth for more insight into those unseen aspects of our present nature that are reaping their regrets even as they sow more of the same dark seeds.

2. We must learn to sit quietly with ourselves and wait patiently for the light of God's peace to replace those dark, noisy thoughts and feelings telling us that we have too much *old baggage* to make the journey home. Each time we sow these seeds through some quiet meditation, we reap the strength that comes from realizing that this silence that comes to us is our true home.

3. We must deliberately remember our intention to start our whole life over every moment we awaken to find ourselves reliving some past conflict. To cultivate this refreshed outlook, born of remembering that our true life is always new in the Now, is to let go of who we have been and to begin reaping a life free of anger and fear.

4. We must learn to look our fears, weariness, and anxiety directly in the eye, and instead of seeing what is impossible according to *their* view of life, sow the seeds of a new self by daring to doubt their dark view of things. Our refusal to identify with self-limiting negative states reaps us the reward of rising above their inherent limitations.

Here is the key lesson of this study section: It is not enough to just sow seeds in this physical life, i.e., struggle for or make millions, invent the greatest gizmo ever, become the who's who of some social registry, for regardless of how sublime these intentions first seem, and even if their seeds should grow and flourish, they can only grow into forms that pass and fall in time. If we wish a life that is whole and loving, one that is filled with new light, then we must sow these eternal seeds within ourselves; that is our work. Make your own list of ways to work at sowing the seeds of the higher life. Set your self to the task of being an inwardly awake person and watch how you begin to reap the awareness that makes all things possible.

FIND PERSONAL FREEDOM
IN THE PRINCIPLES OF INVISIBLE JUSTICE

Letting go is the glad discovery that regardless of who, or what, we may have struggled with in our past, already in our hands is the power we need to free ourselves from what once held us down. Through our studies we have learned how any discouraging thought can be dropped as soon as we recognize that it's a lie. We have discovered that stressful negative states have no authority over us other than what we lend to them in our spiritual sleep. Now it's time for us to learn another great lesson of self-liberation: how to let go of our disappointments with other people, including our wish to punish them for any pain or sorrow we may still feel due to our relationship with them. This brings us to a key lesson in letting go.

We can never hope to be free as long as any part of us struggles with, or suffers over what others are doing, have done, or won't do with their lives. Besides, if we could remain aware of the often-compromised state of our own character, that is, how we still do those things to others that we don't want to do, this awakened conscience would stir in us a new need. Rather than worrying about whether so-and-so gets his comeuppance for being the kind of person he is, our attention would be elsewhere. It would be focused fully upon being in the Now of our own life wherein we would be actively attending to what we must do to let go of old resentments that won't let go of us!

A great part of our inability to release this conflict-bred sense of feeling ourselves to be a hostage of how others behave is born of a mistaken perception. In our ignorance, we believe we must fix others who have done us wrong, otherwise justice won't be served. But, as we are about to thankfully discover, the truth is far from this popular view and the chain of victims it serves to create.

As our study of the Invisible Eternals reveals, there are great powers at work around and within us all the time. And as we awaken to realize that these same perfect principles are already in place to empower us, this same understanding puts us in relationship with a whole new order of freedom. As we learned in Chapter Four, freedom is not a creation of ours. It is not something attained by making life line up with our wishes; it is a system already in place, needing only our awareness of its abiding reality to realize its power as our own. These same invisible laws hold true when it comes to justice for all. We've all heard the phrase, "What goes around comes around." This principle of karma, that what we give, we will receive in return, is a mathematical law whose root runs through the heart of reality. Our present problem is that we don't understand this principle in operation because we can't always see with our physical eyes its unfailing fruition. But be assured, what is evil in nature never goes without its reward, just as what is good is always rewarded in kind.

With these truths in mind, how many of us spend our precious time and energy fuming over what others may have done to us? Unseen in the steam of our heated emotions and churning thoughts is the one inescapable fact that we are the secret prisoner of anyone we wish to punish. And the more we would punish this person, the less freedom we have to be at peace with ourselves.

Here's a beautiful lesson in invisible justice, followed by an explanation that will help you let go of any revenge-filled, self-tangling thought. We need never concern ourselves with whether or not some wrongdoer will get his just due. Here's why: *any person who does wrong to another is already punished*. More correctly stated, anyone who acts unjustly in life instantaneously ensures that he or she will be corrected by the celestial laws that govern all such trespasses. It doesn't matter one bit that you or I don't see this law enacted to our satisfaction. The fact remains: an invisible justice system already exists. This means we need never judge anyone, nor wish some sentence of suffering upon him or her. This understanding is a gift of great freedom known only by the true few. And we can count ourselves among these liberated ones if we are willing to learn what we must. Here are a few vital facts about this unseen system that ensures equality for all.

Around and within us reside invisible and powerful laws that rule over reality in all its infinite forms. These forces of instant righteousness, or perfect balance if you prefer, are always at work. Nothing escapes their imperceptible presence; everything yields to the weight of their judgment.

One reason many of us fail to recognize the existence of this celestial justice always acting upon us in the Now—or find solace in its perpetual sovereignty—is because of our conditioning: we just aren't comfortable with the idea of any other order of rectitude apart from exacting the proverbial *pound of flesh*. But here is just one small example of how these perfect laws—in one even motion—sentence those who trespass, while liberating those who realize them: *All pretense punishes the pretender.* Here is proof of this truth. The smallest act of cunning on our part always starts with secret self-conflict.

Other truths that are the foundation of justice are all around us if we know where to look within ourselves. For example, *Any embraced hatred festers the heart of the one holding this sickness.* Here's another principle governed by these same laws, a principle that allows us to pity those who blindly accumulate power or possessions at the cost of a greater good: *the seed of any greed always lies within some self-compromising fear, so that nothing can be won by its actions that doesn't frighten us further.*

These next truths are also part of this same system of justice. It is our growing insight into these incorruptible laws that shows us the wisdom in the timeless idea of *letting go and letting God.*

The love of God transforms all things bitter into something better.

Self-correction is instant self-elevation.

All of these truths—along with their exciting implications—prove the existence of a great and universal system of invisible justice that upholds the laws of the Invisible Eternals. And if we look deeper still into the heart of these new discoveries, we will find within them the promise of this welcome relief: we are forever *relieved* of the conflict and misery of wanting to penalize those who may have caused us pain. We can let go of all forms of lashing out at others because we see the truth of how things actually work. Getting wrongly caught up in the conflict of wanting to fix the bad behavior of someone else only opens the door and invites other problems and pain into our own life!

Now we can leave these people alone to their own trials and torment, for we have seen that their negative nature is one and the same as their punishment; and further we have seen that whatever weight we would try to add on to their backs only falls onto our own. To act from this higher self-awareness not only helps free us from the initial pain born of a negative reaction to what others have done to us, but it also keeps us from wrongly investing ourselves in trying to correct what is already in the throes of being corrected! And once we stop locking ourselves up with wasted judgments and their attendant, never-ending worries, we find that not only are we free, but that there's no power in the universe capable of holding us captive again.

FIND THE MISSING HALF
OF WHAT YOU NEED TO FULFILL YOURSELF

QUESTION: One thing has always troubled me about trying to live in the sheltering safety of the Now. I know these eternal principles are real and powerful in themselves, but when it comes to making them actually *work* for me it's like trying to mold sunlight into a lantern that I can carry around in my hand. I know I must be missing something, but I don't know what to look for—let alone where to begin my search!

ANSWER: In the apocryphal gospel of St. Thomas, Christ is quoted as saying to his disciples, "If you will only receive what is in your sight, what is hidden will become clear to you." Can it really be that simple? Let's look at one of these eternal principles that runs, unseen by most of us, right through the heart of Now. To catch a glimpse of its perpetual presence in our life is to realize the power we need to let go and live without fear in the present moment.

On some days more than others—though it's never truly absent from us—we have all felt a certain emotion best described as the feeling that something is missing from our life. This unwanted, sometimes haunting, state of self is no respecter of occasion; it can appear almost anytime, even in the midst of one's own birthday party! And just like those trick birthday candles that can't be blown out, but reignite themselves after only a moment passes, nothing we do seems able to extinguish this recurring ache. The truth is . . . we *are* missing something vital, something that's not only essential for our own happiness, but something crucial to the fulfillment of our soul itself.

We are missing out on at least fifty percent of our own life! Let me restate this unseen fact about our present state of being, using different words to convey the same important idea: Over half of what happens to each of us throughout the course of our life is unwanted by us, refused in one way or another, and what is rejected by us is as good as going missing. What is this missing half? The following short story will reveal the surprising answer, and then we will examine its lessons to help us realize how we can turn its timeless principles into true spiritual power.

Long, long ago, in a time before the world was the way we now experience it, there was an earlier world. It was filled with conditions and creatures still being formed by invisible forces that were as seeds to these new creations in much the same way as the seeds we know today are to the fruits and flowers to which they give rise.

It was the Age of Formation. Everything was as it should be. Each creature and its living condition was something new and unique, the true first of its kind. And all the creatures that followed would bear the mark of their predecessor's experience, born of its relationship with this new world. Everything was good. Only not all the creatures knew this. And that's where our story begins.

The first great Blue Salamander was clearly disturbed. After all, so many things seemed wrong: From the moment she became conscious of herself in this strange world, the sun was too hot for her tender skin, and the uneven surface of the great rock she stood upon hurt her newly formed feet. But that wasn't the worst of it. She instinctively knew that she was only one of many first creatures lurking around the shore of this first great lake, and that some of her neighbors wanted her for their potential first meal! Yet, as challenging as these physical conditions may have been, they were really the least of her troubles. There was something else.

Her growing sense of being so exposed to the elements was heightened by the fear she felt having to live out in the open. But, the only other option available to her—apart from sitting there in plain sight of who knows what predator—was to slip into the dark waters lapping up against the rock beneath her—something she was strangely drawn to do, but whose very thought terrified her!

In truth, she had no idea what the nature of these waters were, let alone what would happen to her should she accidentally fall into them. So she did the only thing she could. She continued to loudly complain about the harshness of life in this new world, hoping against hope that something might change. A moment later, it did.

Fortunately for her, because she never heard the first great Golden Ram as he came up behind, he was only looking to find out why she was making such a racket. In fact, so consumed was she with the sound of her own complaints that when he spoke up at last and broke her monologue, she nearly jumped clean out of her own skin!

"Excuse me," he said, "but why all the commotion? Don't you know that you're breaking the First Silence? Not to mention," he continued, as he looked left and right around where they stood, "that you are drawing to yourself what will no doubt prove to be a lot of unwanted attention!"

She spun in her tracks and looked up to see a mighty form standing right over her, but from his gentle expression she instantly realized there was nothing to fear from this golden creature with such great horns. The words that came pouring out of her mouth sounded more like a confession than the start of a casual conversation, but she didn't care.

"I'm sick and tired of being scared," she said. Then, sensing that he might understand what she herself had yet to, she added, "And I am running out of hope. I've searched and searched, and there is no shelter or safety for me anywhere." Her last few words were spoken so softly as to be lost in the gentle sound of the waters ebbing up on the shore. "I fear there is none to be found."

"Well," the great Ram snorted the first snort that startled both of them, "I see how you might feel that way, but there's no reason for that." He shook his great head back and forth as if to confirm his own thinking and repeated himself once more: "No, there's no reason at all."

She tried to look into his eyes to get the meaning of what he was saying, but his gaze seemed to be set upon something beyond her. Then, a moment later, without waiting to hear what she thought of his assessment, he walked off into the distance.

To the great Salamander this was insult to injury, and had she the time, there's little doubt she would have made the First Mountain out of the First Molehill; but a heartbeat later came the First Nightfall, and darkness wrapped all of creation in an unknown blanket. Unable to see now, a deep tremble passed through her. Not only did she feel herself to be in imminent danger, but in what direction could she possibly move without further endangering herself? What other choice did she have? A strong resolve stirred in her, and drawing in the deepest breath she knew how, she took a running leap.

It was several days later when the Golden Ram again wandered back by the sunbaked rock where he first met the great Blue Salamander. And as he approached there was a detectable lightness to his gait, for during his travels he had been a grateful witness to countless wonders unfolding in this early chapter of life. And now his hope was that the great Salamander had herself been taken through some of these monumental changes. He had his answer the moment her saw her contentedly sunning herself on the great rock.

"Well," he said, "don't you look happy? If I didn't know better, I'd swear you weren't the same great Blue Salamander I met here sometime ago!"

She smiled back at him to confirm her identity, but both of them knew the truth. He went on, "So, what happened to you? You're looking so happy and at peace with your new home."

She lifted herself up a bit and turned slightly to better face him. Even though she suspected he already knew her story, she wanted to see the expression on his golden face as he listened to what had happened to her. Drawing in a deep breath she said, "Well, as best I know how to describe it . . . I drowned."

"You did *what*? " he blurted out in a kind of mock shock. "How is that possible when here you are right before me, looking more alive than the first time I met you?"

The Salamander scrutinized his semi-serious expression to confirm her earlier intuition that he was well ahead of her story, but she continued on anyway in the light spirit of the moment they were sharing.

"Wild, isn't it?" she beamed back at him, and he nodded his great head as she kept talking. "Anyway, here's what happened. Almost as soon as you left me in the heat of that first terrible day, everything within *and* around me turned totally dark. I felt so alone, afraid, and completely at a loss about my own future that I didn't know what to do. The only thing I could think was that I was going to die for sure. So rather than just sit there, helpless, waiting for the inevitable, I took things into my own hands."

She drew another breath and the great Ram could see that she was now reliving the event. "I gathered myself up and, with a running jump, I leaped as far as I could out into the heart of the waters before me."

She paused for a moment and then spoke in a less excited voice, "I sank straight to the bottom like a stone!"

"What happened then?"

"It's funny," she said, "because I sat down there in the cold darkness and held my breath as long as I could, basically just waiting for the end to come."

"An*d*?" he prompted her to get to the point. "Get on with it, will you!"

She smiled again. "That's the point. It *didn't*! It was amazing," she let out a burst of enthusiasm. "There came this moment when, finally, I had no choice left but to draw in a breath. To my complete astonishment, I could breathe as easily under the water as I am able to do here on the surface with you!"

She could see by his return smile that he knew perfectly well what she had gone through. And though she was sure he already knew exactly how she felt, she finished her story as a way of saying thanks.

"And now I feel at home in whichever of the two worlds I happen to be visiting."

This brief story illustrates a much more significant spiritual lesson. Just as our amphibious heroine discovered that she was, in fact, a creature of two worlds—capable of breathing both air and water—and that she need no longer live with the fear born of existing in only one world, *so too is our True Nature created to dwell in two worlds.*

KEYS TO CLAIMING YOUR CELESTIAL BIRTHRIGHT

On one hand we are made to live out our physical existence in the world of passing time. This is the world we are all familiar with. It is the realm in which we experience the birth and death of everything from the most mundane of our interests—those passions that come and go—all the way up to and including our lives themselves. Our physical being is carried along in an invisible stream of time whose never-ending twists and turns bring us headlong into the uncertainty that this level of self must seemingly endure. But we also have another nature—one that entitles us, *if* we will claim this celestial birthright, to live in another world through which this stream of time runs. This other world is the invisible realm of the *timeless Now.*

Awakening to this timeless birthright of ours grants us the precious gift of being able to see that our present worries and fears are nothing more than the negative results of mistaking ourselves to be something far less than what we are in reality. But before we can hope to realize our place in this secret shelter, hidden in our own higher consciousness, there is some specialized interior work to be done. As the late, great author Vernon Howard taught his students, "We are meant to have the best of *both* worlds, but instead we have the worst of one . . . and none of the other!" Our task, if we wish to awaken to the fearless life, is to find out why this insight is true.

This chapter began with the assertion that we are missing out on at least fifty percent of our lives. Now let's see if we can prove the truth behind this surprising idea. Virtually the last thing that any of us wants to have happen in the course of life is for something that we care about *to come to an end* before we are through with it. In other words, pretty much the only time we willingly consent to something ending in our life is when our interests in it have dried up or moved on to something new and more exciting.

However, the overwhelming evidence is that Real Life works differently. Clearly reality isn't concerned that we don't like the way it runs its invisible timetable. In spite of our desires, things end when *their* time comes, not when we say the time is right. And if the main lesson hasn't touched home yet—fully half of the Great Circle of Life, including our part of it, is filled with the end of things.

So, to rephrase a statement made at the outset of this chapter: *at least half of our life is spent not wanting our own life*, which means we are effectively missing out on half of our lives! But *why* is it like this? Must it continue to be so? What is it about the end of things in our life that some part of us finds so terrible that, half of our life experience ends up being rejected—literally thrown away? See if the following explanation helps to solve this mysterious condition.

The reason we resist virtually all endings in our life—wherein we feel as though something has been wrongfully taken away from us—is because these same unwanted moments leave us feeling terribly *empty* inside ourselves. In truth, it is this overwhelming sense of emptiness that we detest, and not the changing condition itself that we so habitually protest. So when things naturally come to a close in life, our pain isn't so much born of the fact that something now ends, as it is that *within this moment of ending* we are forced to meet a certain order of emptiness in us for which we are just not prepared. We are brought face to face with a great void in the center of our heart that we thought had been filled. And then we make this common, but largely unrealized mistake:

When faced with the prospect of living with an emptiness that seems capable of swallowing us whole, most of us elect to do the only thing we believe is possible under such dire circumstances. We start right away working out fresh ways to fill ourselves once more. The drill is familiar: find someone or something new with which to make another beginning. Do whatever is needed to bring an end to the emptiness. There's only one small problem with these solutions: *they don't work!* That is unless we believe that being compelled to fill a hole in our soul over and over again is the same as being whole.

You may be wondering, "If I don't take action to end to my sense of emptiness, what am I going to do? If I don't make effort, then how am I going to make myself feel whole?" From evidence gleaned from our own life experiences, the following answer ought to ring true: When it comes to experiencing an overall sense of peace, happiness, and abiding contentment, we are not created to be self-filling beings. Instead, we need to realize that self-wholeness appears *by itself* within us.

Much in the same way as a sunbaked field of wild flowers has as its only balm the spring rains, so, too, does each season of our emptiness have but one true solution: the stirring touch of that Celestial Life that seeded us with this sense of emptiness in the first place. Why are we created to experience such a seemingly bottomless emptiness in the center of ourselves? Because in coming to know this dark half of the Living Light's great unseen life, we might—of our own free will—learn to quench our thirst—fill ourselves with those life-giving waters that are ever-streaming out of its eternal source.

Our True Self is, in part, a secret field where a never-ending cycle of ebb and flow plays itself out in passing expressions of alternating fullness and emptiness, much as runoff winter waters from great mountains rush down to fill valley lakes parched dry by the passage of summer.

But the greater part of our Original Self is to these mountains and their valley lakes as is the whole of that countryside in which these same landmarks dwell, for even though the round of seasons come and go, causing endless changes *within* it, nothing really changes *about* it. Our True Nature lives in the ever-changing, yet never-changing Now; that vast country of higher consciousness wherein we are empowered to welcome all forms of fullness *and* emptiness as our friends, instead of mistaking ourselves a friend of one and foe of the other.

If we would awaken to a conscious relationship with these ever-flowing forces that are the lifeblood of our True Nature, and if we are to realize that this awareness alone can free us of our fear of being empty, then what is asked of us becomes clear: we must stop trying to create conditions for ourselves through which we hope to escape the fear of our own emptiness. We must willingly slip into these seemingly dark waters of ourselves, where, if we will wait there quietly enough, we will awaken to find ourselves in the higher atmosphere of a new world. For our spiritual daring, we will gain an intimate knowledge of these invisible eternal forces at work within us; one emptying us, even as another moves into its place to fill that open space with its new and unmistakable presence. If these words sound promising, it's because they are. As this priceless self-knowledge born of higher self-awareness grows in us, we will realize that the freedom we seek is found everywhere and all at once. We will no longer fear the end of things because at last we have seen that within ourselves, the truth of who we really are is as endless as the beginning of life.

ASK THE MASTERS

QUESTION: Why struggle, as you suggest, trying to discover and understand these invisible eternal forces when the world we already see and know is so full of possibilities?

ANSWER: *One drop of eternity is of greater weight than a vast ocean of finite things.*

—Karl Barth

QUESTION: What can I expect to happen once I begin letting go and living in the Now? What happens when I practice this interior work of allowing myself to be filled, instead of always trying to fill myself?

ANSWER: *The moment we make up our mind that we are going on with this determination to exact God over all, we step out of the world's parade. We shall acquire a new viewpoint; a new and different psychology will be formed within us; a new power will begin to surprise us by its upsurging and its out-going.*

—A. W. Tozer

KEY LESSONS IN REVIEW

1. Whenever we do the very best we can and give the very most that we have to give, even though we may be far from perfect in that moment, that moment is acting upon us to bring us into its native perfection. It is only through learning to endure our own imperfections that we realize that Perfection itself is our guide and master.

2. If we ask, "What did I do to deserve this?" it shows we have forgotten that we ask for what we receive with every thought and feeling we embrace. Our attention animates, and thereby grants life to all that we hold in mind, just as the plant always reveals the type of seed sown.

3. Just as the sun rises to fill a darkened morning with its soft new light, so too does the Living Light of Truth descend into the willing soul, transforming its earthen elements into a spiritual temple

ablaze with God's eternal light.

4. Nothing in the universe can interfere with the will to be free. This means that for those of us who would know freedom, our part is not to struggle with what we perceive as our captor, but rather to learn to act within the nature of that Sovereign Self we would be. For when we assume the Character of Freedom, we become possessed with its powers. We win its liberated state and are lifted high above the reach of any self-wrecking state.

5. When we realize, at last, that there is no place in life toward which we are racing that is not already disappearing, and that there is no place where one willingly remains that isn't beginning anew within itself, then will we have at last arrived where our heart longs to be.

CHAPTER EIGHT

Advanced Lessons in Letting Go

What could be more natural than letting go? Think about it. If, as we discussed in the last chapter, half of our life is spent meeting moments that are natural endings, then what are we to do with these things in our lives that can no longer serve us in a meaningful way? The answer? We must let them go! To do anything else would be unnatural, even unhealthy for us.

Imagine a tree that has become so identified with its own green leaves that when the first chill of fall touches its limbs, this tree decides it wants to hold onto what it already has. "After all," the tree reasons, "what if spring doesn't bring me something at least as good as what I have now? Why should I let go?" Of course, come the winter snows, this tree that held on so dearly to its summer leaves, cracks and breaks beneath the weight of a stressful load it was never intended to carry. The moral of this little story is simple: We are not created to walk around with the weight of the world—all our experiences, memories, and past—on our shoulders.

Letting go is the out-breath of the universe. It is part of a natural cycle connected to a greater whole, where the ending of anything already has a new beginning built into it. And just as we must expel a breath before we draw in the new air that revitalizes our physical system, so too we must learn to let go of whatever compromises the natural wholeness of our Original Self if we wish to realize its native spiritual contentment.

What are we actually talking about when we speak of letting go? After all, no one wants to let go of something that has proven itself to be satisfying! Whatever it is that we wish to let go of must be something from which we wish to be free. This may be unpleasant or troubling relationships, a problem-filled past or fearful future, any form of addiction, recent painful events—or any of those disturbing thoughts and feelings about these same troubling things that we no longer want in our lives.

The truth is that troubles like these come with being human. We all know how it feels *to want* to let go. The problem is that wanting to let go, and actually being able to, is still light years apart for most of us. But it need not remain this way. The gulf can be sealed permanently once we understand that all that separates us from our intention to let go are those mistaken ideas we carry around about the nature of what's actually weighing us down. This is why we need new and higher self-knowledge.

For instance, no thing in itself—no event, no relationship, no regret-filled thought or feeling—has any real weight of its own with which to pull us down. The nature of what really weighs on us is something altogether different. This can help to explain a deep mystery: Why is it that regardless of everything we do in our exterior life to rid ourselves of this or that problem, person, or contrary condition, we have yet to genuinely shake ourselves free? The answer begins with this next insight.

The real act of letting go is first an interior action, followed, if needful, by a wiser exterior action. After all, what is it that binds us if not where we are blind to some unconscious need to either maintain or keep forming these painful attachments? To see the truth of these findings is to realize why there can be no substitute for self-illumination. After all, no one frees themselves by laying down with one hand what they unknowingly cling to with the other! This explains why the aim of all true spiritual teachings has always had a dual purpose: 1) to reveal to us that no condition in our life exists apart from the consciousness responsible for its continuing creation, and 2) to bring the light of this higher self-knowledge into the unexamined darkness of our consciousness so that we no longer make the mistake of clinging to anything that compromises our integrity.

A special short story will help shed more light on this part of our advanced study in letting go. Its happy ending will teach us all we need to know about how to drop any dark state that would try to drag us under.

TAKE CONSCIOUS COMMAND OF THE FORCES THAT MANIFEST YOUR LIFE

It had been an unusual summer, full of storms and quirky squalls, which appeared out of nowhere, and many of the fishermen living along the coast were having their share of difficulties. The story was the same for Hans and his family.

Hans's father and his father before him had spent their days netting small fish from the productive shoals just off the rocky shores of their native country. But this was the worst weather in recent history, and everyone whose livelihood depended upon the bounty of the seas was suffering the same fate. You could set out in the morning after a red sky at night (a sailor's delight), and from out of nowhere would appear a storm that not only made fishing impossible in shallow waters, but could also easily capsize small dories loaded down with their acre of nets.

Times were hard for Hans and all the other fishermen in his village, except one: the crazy old man who lived by himself in Crystal Cove. The cove was a small, secluded inlet around the point, hidden from view by tall, craggy rocks. Every day, despite unfavorable weather, the old fisherman would roll his wooden cart into the village, filled to the brim with his catch of the day! And he was never without an old straw sun hat, even on cold foggy days.

As you might imagine, gossip was rampant. Some took him to be a wizard of a sort. And even though most of the men wanted to learn how he always managed to net fish when no one else even dared launch their boat, most folks thought the old fellow had spent one too many days in the sun, so no one troubled him much. One day, after a series of fierce squalls that had made fishing impossible, Hans woke early to try and get out to sea before the winds kicked up again. But he no more raised the sail on his dory than in rolled the signs of another approaching storm. He threw up his hands into the air and cried out, "Why?"

A moment later a thought came to him and, before he knew it, he was out of the boat headed in the direction of Crystal Cove, where the wild old fisherman lived. Perhaps he wasn't as mad as the villagers thought him to be; maybe he just knew something no one else did. There was only one way to find out. Ten minutes later, just as he crested the great rock outcrop overlooking Crystal Cove, the approaching storm plowed into the coast.

With the rains coming in almost sideways, Hans thought maybe he ought to abandon his plan and head back home. His mind tormented him as he stood there in the freezing wind; after all, how stupid can you get to even think of visiting this old man, let alone to knock on his shanty door in the throes of a storm like this? But just as he began to turn in his tracks, his eyes caught sight of something his mind couldn't explain. He squinted to keep the blowing rain out of his eyes, but there was no mistaking it. About three hundred yards offshore, bounced around by angry white-capped waves, was the old man's small dory. Hans looked again to be certain, and sure enough, not only was that the old man's dory out there, but the old man was in it.

"What in the world?" Hans blurted out involuntarily. He leaned forward to try and see better what he simply couldn't believe. Right in the midst of the storm-tossed ocean it looked as if the old fisherman was having a nap! And then, as if to confirm what seemed so inconceivable, a second later the old man stood straight up in the dory, stretched out his legs, and made a great big yawn, like he had just stepped out of his bed after a good night's sleep! But this was just the beginning of a scene that Hans would never forget.

The next moment the old man raised both his arms and held them there, suspended above his head. Hans wondered what in the world was he up to now. A second later he found out. Just as the old man slowly lowered his arms to his side, the storm around his little boat began to subside. A moment later, dark skies gave way to sunlight. A shudder went through Hans. How could this be? He wanted to run in two directions at once, away from this miracle and toward it; but he stayed right where he was because, a heartbeat later, something equally unlikely took place before his unbelieving eyes.

The old man reached down, picked up his tattered net, and threw it out into the now-quieted waters. Before it could sink out of sight, dozens of fish began jumping into it. The old fisherman smiled and pulled in his catch, but Hans was no longer watching. He was headed as fast as he could to get down to the rough-hewn dock where he knew the old man would soon return to tie up his boat.

Hans arrived, just as the old man was pulling alongside the dock, and caught the worn rope that was thrown to him so that he might help make fast the craft. They exchanged brief smiles, but no words were exchanged. Together, still silent, they unloaded the catch. Then Hans could be quiet no longer.

"Sir," he spoke, wanting to be as polite as possible. "Please forgive me, but I *must* know . . . " He stopped himself midstream, hearing the demanding tone that had slipped into his voice. Something deep within him told him this was not the right way to speak to any man with the powers he had just seen displayed. So he took a deep breath and started over.

"You must understand, I give you my word that I wasn't spying on you; I only came here to ask you for some advice on foul-weather fishing. But when I arrived, you were already anchored out there." Hans pointed in the direction of the open sea. He took in another deep breath and continued.

"The truth is you were caught out in a storm that would have taken most boats right to the ocean's floor." He paused for a moment to consider the impossibility of what he knew he was going to say next: "But instead of sinking into the churning waters, I watched you calm them!"

Searching for any sign that he may have misread the event he just described, Hans looked, for the first time, directly into the old fisherman's eyes. They were a light gray-blue with a watery depth of their own, and he felt drawn to their stillness, like someone who comes upon a hidden reflecting pond and longs to know its secret. The old man spoke and broke the spell.

"Oh that," he said, as if he describing his old straw sun hat. "Yes, I guess I must have dozed off for a moment, because that storm sure came out of nowhere. But then again," he paused like he was chewing over a thought that he must have found funny because he finished it with a chuckle, "seems like storms always do that, don't they son?"

Hans didn't laugh. He couldn't. Was this old fisherman playing with him? Surely he had to know that the power to calm a storm was no laughing matter. Best to just say what was on his mind, he thought to himself, let the cards fall where they will. As the words began to tumble from his mouth, he realized that he didn't have the courage he felt only a moment before. The best he could manage was, "But *how* did you do that?" and he pointed again out to the now-quieted ocean waters, hoping his gesture explained what he couldn't find the words for.

"Oh that," said the old man for the second time. "Well, as I told you before, I must have fallen asleep and the storm caught me off-guard. So there I was and the . . . " But Hans couldn't wait anymore, and cut him off.

"I know *that* much, sir," Hans implored him; "But what I don't know is how you were able to calm the storm and keep it from swamping your boat? If I could only understand such powers I could always provide for my family. I would be the happiest man on earth, I am sure of it! Won't you tell me your secret, please?"

"Well, son, if you'd just get ahold of your britches, that's what I'm trying to tell you. When you first saw me I had fallen asleep in my boat, something you never want to do when you're out at sea. But the moment I woke up and realized where I was, well I knew at once that storm had nothing to do with me."

Hans moved his head forward and tilted it slightly to one side to indicate he was waiting for the old man to finish this strange explanation, but nothing else followed. "And . . . ?" Hans said when he couldn't wait any longer, leaning his head even farther forward.

"And *what*, boy?" said the old man. "What else do you need to know? When you understand that these storms have nothing to do with *you*, well then . . . Don't you see?" and he waved his hand like his was shooing away a bothersome fly . . . "You just take yourself out of them."

"How is that possible?" asked Hans.

The old man studied his eyes for a moment and decided the boy was sincere. He had already started walking back up the path toward his home when he turned back and said, "All right then," he said. "Come along, and don't be slow about it! And don't forget to bring the fish with you. We'll see if we can't teach you a thing or two about how to dismiss storms."

Over the months and years that followed, Hans and the old man of the sea became fast friends. Slowly, surely, Hans came to know what his heart longed to understand.

And if we could have listened to their quiet conversations as they walked the beach or mended their nets together, this is the secret we would have learned regarding all mental and emotional storms, regardless of their size: No disturbance of any kind has the power to swamp and sink our heart or mind once we realize that we are the one lending these storms the force they need to drag us down. In practical terms this means that whatever disturbances we unknowingly create within us may be instantly *un-created* in the very same moment we withdraw our consent to remain conflicted. With this spiritually empowering idea in mind, let's continue to gather the facts we need to stop these inner storms in their tracks!

THE POWER TO LEAVE
PAINFUL THOUGHTS AND FEELINGS BEHIND YOU

Just as a storm in the atmosphere of the earth is born of conflicting fronts of different temperatures colliding with one another, so too must there be conflicting forces within us in order to form a mental or emotional storm. Our task is to become conscious of these unseen forces that dwell in the unenlightened parts of us. As we grow to realize that no disturbance can remain within us without our granting it the force it needs to sustain its fury, we realize that we have at our disposal two great powers. We are empowered to dismiss storms when they appear in our psychic system and, with time and practice, we can learn to dismiss these disturbances before they begin!

What are these invisible conflicting forces at work within us that cause so much foul weather? We uncover the first of these unconscious forces by recognizing that the storms in our lives all share a common cause. Each storm, large or small, centers around something that happens to us that we don't want to be happening for whatever reasons. A few quick examples prove this insight, but best success is assured if you will fill in the blanks from your own experience.

Imagine a woman caught in an emotional firestorm of anger because she does not want to be treated like *that*. Or a man who feels trapped by a tormenting depression because he doesn't want what life continues to bring to him. Can we see that these two storms share a common root? Both rise as they do because of our unconscious resistance to something that has already happened.

Whenever we face an unwanted event and find ourselves feeling nothing but resistance, we can discover that this stress-mess is made from our insistence that this should not have happened. And how about when we recall past mistakes, painfully reliving how we fell down—either a moment ago or ten years back? Aren't we sure that whatever that error may have been—it shouldn't have taken place? Which brings us to the following insight that deserves a few moments extra consideration. It feels natural for us to go along with the feeling of not wanting what our not wanting is powerless to change!

What on earth lies hidden in this strange struggle of ours that compels us to wrestle with what amounts to mental ghosts? After all, once something has happened in our life—that moment is over; it's gone, done with, finished. Clearly, what was no longer exists in the here and Now. So, we have to ask ourselves, given this understanding that is above dispute, how can something from our own past feel as real and as alive as it does to us in the present moment? The following answer brings us one step closer to living in a world without storms.

Within our mind lingers an untold number of chemically and electrically stored images of the way things were. These mental pictures include complete scenes of every experience past, as well as pleasurable images of achievements yet to come. And these same images are secret storehouses of all the sensations that accompanied them in the moment of their creation. Each one is laden with its original emotional content that pours into us each time we revisit them. To help visualize how this unseen psychic sequence unfolds within, put yourself in the place of this imaginary person—Barbara—walking down the street.

As Barbara window-shops on fashionable Seventh Avenue, her eye catches sight of a lace-sleeved lavender blouse on sale in one of her favorite stores. In an instant, Barbara recalls wearing a similar blouse many years ago the night her father passed away. Now, virtually unnoticed, a small wave of regret washes over her. For reasons unknown to her, as she stands there still looking at a blouse she feels sure should be in her closet, she is beginning to think about the last words she had with her father, and how she wishes she would have said something else.

The more Barbara is drawn into these flooding considerations, the more she suffers. And the more unwanted this painful experience becomes, the more she unconsciously resists her mounting turmoil until she is caught in a full-blown storm right on Seventh Avenue! Haven't we all been there before? Where a seemingly harmless thought, which we turn over in our mind, becomes a tornado? Well, it need not be like that . . . for any of us!

Now it's time for us to learn how to dismiss any gathering storm before it sinks us. Recall, if you will, the words of the old man from Crystal Cove to Hans, the would-be fearless fisherman who wanted to know his secret way to dismiss storms. He told the young man, *"That storm has nothing to do with me!"* Here is the secret meaning of his amazing spiritual statement, as well as how we can employ this new knowledge to empower us in our hour of need: The only reason we ever find ourselves caught in a psychological storm is because we have been drawn, without knowing it, into identifying with—actually merging with—mental images from our past. These images are pre-loaded—rather like psychological time capsules—with punishing thoughts and feelings that flood into us the instant we identify with them. As the invisible, but psychically palpable blows from these painful memories pour through on us, we are unconsciously moved to try and resist them—all of which makes us feel as though we are trapped in a storm about which we can do nothing other than try to escape its lashing!

Once we invite the following insight to become our own, we need never again endure the pounding of such negative states: No storm of mental torment or dark, emotional suffering *belongs* to you. Any wave of resentment, anxiety, or fear that comes to wash you away is nothing more than a kind of psychic residue left over from who you once were. Not only do these negative states have nothing in common with your True Nature, but they cannot enter into the living Now where this higher consciousness lives.

This same truth can be said in a slightly different way: we cannot be punished by any painful storm when we are grounded in the present moment. The reason for this perfect protection is as pure as it is simple: Psychological storms are powerless to push their divisive and destructive forces into the spiritual harbor of Now because, within its native wholeness, they have no way to remain there. Now let's pull these important lessons together in a short summary.

We have seen that the storms we suffer are not born simply from any particular event that takes place, but rather they rise from an unknown ground in us due to our undetected resistance to them. Further, these unwanted events that we so strongly resist are not the actual events themselves. What we secretly struggle against in these moments are unwanted images of that event fashioned by ourselves. This occurs, for example, when we imagine a fearful future, or see ourselves thrown for a social loss of some sort. In these moments we suffer, as we do, because we are looking at what we don't want to see. And then, because we don't know that we have been tricked into giving these negative fantasies our attention, we try to imagine ways to escape their punishing presence. The more we struggle to get away, the more attention we inadvertently lend to what we wish would disappear! It's a great paradox: not wanting to look upon what is bothering us keeps what is bothering us in plain view! But now we are beginning to see our way out of this trap.

From this moment forward, whenever some dark storm appears in us we must neither run from it, nor stand there and hate what we think is happening. Instead we must awaken to ourselves, bring ourselves back into the Now and quietly, deliberately, drop any image that our thought-nature presents within us to justify the brewing conflict. Learning to dismiss the storms that sink our chances to be happy takes dedicated inner work, but you may be assured such powers are possible. Your True Nature already dwells beyond the reach self-wrecking storms. Join it; begin Now!

TEN WORDS TO HELP YOU LET GO OF ANY NEGATIVE STATE

Nothing seems harder to accept than some of these spiritual facts to which we are awakening. After all, who would ever believe that we are responsible for so much of what proves to be unnecessary suffering? But we are beginning to learn, with the help of honest self-investigation, that we must challenge this involuntary, often intractable refusal to consider such ideas. The truth is that we are actively involved with unseen thoughts and feelings that compromise us. Without the self-knowledge we need to nullify this conflicted condition in our psyche, how can we hope to end the heartaches that begin there? How can we hope to heal something we won't even look at!

On the other hand, nothing is healthier for us than the beautiful process of awakening to how we have been unwittingly involved in our own suffering. We stand in good company when we consent to see these truths within ourselves. All truth teachings agree: freedom from compulsive or otherwise self-wrecking behavior begins with recognizing that we have been unknowingly serving what makes us suffer. Yes, awakening to what has been an unseen conflict in us is a challenge, but this interior work of self-realization is more than offset by the rewards gained for our efforts. Here's why:

Conscious awareness of ourselves is one and the same as living in the Now. It is the seed of a new action whose flowering is a self-wholeness that is inseparable from the higher freedom we seek. Let's examine some evidence to help support these new ideas.

If you watch animals in the wild, one thing is obvious: The nature of an animal and its natural experience of life are indivisibly related. For example, deer attract biting flies. In the high heat of summer you won't see one without the other, and I have seen deer driven nearly crazy by these pests. They have no choice but to suffer this seasonal torment. An animal's nature attracts to it the elements that define its life. I make this point because the same holds true in many ways for human beings. Not only does our present nature attract what we call our life experience, but it also determines the way in which we see and experience these same events.

We may doubt this timeless truth—that one's inner nature determines one's experience of the outer life—but the outcome will show that this is true. All of us know what it's like to find ourselves in a swarm of stinging thoughts and feelings born of past painful experiences and other disheartening regrets and be unable to outrun them or otherwise escape their punishing presence, save in a moment here and there of some pleasurable respite. But this is where the similarity to our animal brothers and sisters ends, or at least where it ought to. An animal has no choice but to tolerate what its nature attracts to it from the world around it. We alone may choose what we receive from life—that is, providing we awaken to reclaim our True Nature.

Most of us have felt, somewhere along the line of our life, a silent prompting to realize the truth of ourselves, even though we may not have recognized it as such. For instance, at some point we have all felt, intuitively if nothing else, that we are not created to live with mental torment of any kind—that we are meant to be more than hapless victims forced to yield to passing conditions. And as we shall see, this is a true intuition.

We are not made by that Great Intelligence that balances whole star systems, to suffer from the conflict that arises from an unbalanced understanding of our own essential nature! This is why if we ever wish to gain conscious control over our present nature—along with what it attracts into our life—we must gain what the great saints and mystics have always held in the highest esteem: true self knowledge. But this needed higher knowledge cannot be acquired from sources outside of us; it must be gained through personal self-discovery. Only real changes in the level of self-understanding can help us effect real changes in our present nature, for the two are very much related. Change one and we change the other, including what it has been attracting into our lives.

The odds favor that we know people whose unconscious thoughts and feelings serve to attract painful events into their lives. More often than not, these people blame their unhappiness on other people or on a world set against them. But higher understanding allows us to see the real reason for their continued misfortune, as well as a spiritual remedy for it. The simple illustration that follows not only sheds more light on this situation, but also serves to prove the main point of this part of our study: *the degree to which we empower ourselves to see what is real, is the same degree to which we are at once set free from the grip of painful illusions that otherwise would imprison us.*

Imagine a young child alone in a darkened bedroom at night. (If you can call on your own past experience, better yet!) A truck drives by, headed down the neighborhood street, and its bright lights pass through the bedroom window—causing a large shadow to suddenly appear on the opposing wall. The child, awakened by the truck as it rumbles by, opens his eyes to see a menacing dark shape race from one corner of the room to the other. And because he witnesses what he does not yet understand, his tender mind is flooded with the fear of monsters. An instant later, an involuntary yelp jumps from his mouth.

Hearing the child cry out, his parents rush into the barely lit room where they quickly surmise what has shaken their son. A moment later they work together to explain the truth of what has happened. His father is the first to speak.

"Son, what you saw dive into that dark corner and disappear is nothing more than a shadow. And while shadows look real, they have no real substance of their own, so they can't hurt you. Would you like Mom and me to prove this to you?" The small child gives a tentative nod of approval.

After turning off the lamp light by the bed, his father turns on a small flashlight and uses it to backlight his hand. The same instant a creepy shadow appears on the distant wall. Then he says to his son, "Okay, here we go; watch closely now; your mother and I are about to show you some real magic!"

Right on cue the child's mother reaches over and flips the switch on the overhead light in the room, and the shadow figure just vanishes. Then, in a light-spirited voice, she picks up where the boy's father had left off.

"Wow! Where did that scary shadow go? Do you see, my darling? A shadow is really just a 'nothing' that only seems real to us because something in us is afraid of it. But now you can see for yourself . . . a shadow simply can't hurt you."

When she sees her child smile back, it's clear that some of the lesson has done its liberating work. And with this both parents kiss him good night, turn off the overhead light, and leave the room with the door slightly open to the hall. And as they return to their room, they smile at one another, knowing that their efforts are the seed of what will bear good fruit. Their child is one step closer to the freedom that comes with understanding scary shadows out of existence.

Just as these attentive parents intend that their child should never again be tormented by the presence of any shadowy shape, so too does the Living Truth hold out a similar instruction for us to take into our hearts and minds. Here is what it would have us hear and understand: *All thoughts are but mere shadows.* They have no substance other than what we impart to them as we see them take shape upon the walls of our own unenlightened mind. One brief example will clarify this last idea.

Take a man who catches a glimpse of a couple ahead of him as they just turn the corner. For a second he thinks he has seen the love of his life walking hand in hand with a complete stranger! Fear and anxiety race through him as he runs to confirm what he's afraid to even imagine. Let's examine this. What this man actually sees in his mind's eye as he sprints to the end of the next corner is not the populated city corner he had seen only the moment before; now he sees virtually nothing other than his own thought-bred tormenting images of what his life will be like once he turns the corner and confirms his worst fear! We all have been caught up in bad dreams such as these.

These emotions of high anxiety feel as real as they do because they are born out of being identified with fear-filled images passing before the mind's eye. These same unwanted images are the negative fabrications of a runaway imagination. They are always a lie. Besides, as it turns out, the woman he saw wasn't his sweetheart after all! But this happy ending is not the point; there's an even happier ending in store for us once we complete this spiritual lesson.

When we think about any painful event, be it three minutes or thirty years old, we look at nothing more than a shadow of what once was—something that is no more! The catch here is that these same thoughts—these shadows of experiences gone by—seem to have a life of their own, and in a way they do, for each carries with it a full complementary set of emotional baggage—the still-smoldering stuff of what we went through the first time the event transpired. To see the truth of this inner dynamic is the first step we must take to learn to walk away from the useless suffering that wrecks our lives, a step that brings us to the essential point of this study.

Whatever the cause, on any given day when life's wheel of fortune takes a bad turn or one's memories go back around to relive some *double zero* day, the pain we feel coursing through us is real in itself, but the actual cause of this suffering is a lie. Can this be? Let's see. One simple question answers this mystery if we will dare answer it as honestly as we know how: if it weren't for something within us wanting to revisit these painful old images—to recall their familiar old pangs—then would we go where this torment is? Surely the answer is *no*! Which brings us the next important question: what is it in our present nature that wants to revisit these shadowy scenes and relive the suffering stored away in them?

We can find the answer to this question when we look at how we habitually react to any form of psychological pain that pops into our awareness. We always try to make the pain go away by looking for the reason it appeared in the first place. But as we are about to discover, our usual behavior here is all a part of our unconscious suffering. Here's why: we are convinced that if we wish to escape our painful state we must somehow find a way to resolve it. This seems to leave us no choice other than to revisit again and again the same unhappy images that gave rise to our pain in the first place! Talk about a vicious circle! This is not unlike getting frightened by a scary scene in a horror movie and then closing our eyes in the hope of escaping the fear we feel for what we have just seen. The more we resist this or any negative image, the more definitively it presses itself into our mind's eye.

But we now know that this pain—along with those unconscious parts of ourselves that have always jumped to answer it—is little more than an echo of a time long gone. As such, we also know how to answer these recurring aches with the only response powerful enough to dissolve them completely. We meet them with our understanding that they no longer have the power to torment us as they have always done.

We are now ready for the next step in learning how to release all that used to make us scared or sad. Our studies have spiritually prepared us for this next important lesson. When we feel some kind of darkness coming over us, we must muster the courage to consciously doubt the reality of this condition, even though our feelings are powerfully trying to convince us that what we feel is true. And we can do this now. We have seen for ourselves that we no longer have to believe in ghosts, let alone the clanking of their chains! Thanks to higher understanding we know better. To help summarize this advanced lesson in letting go, here is a special short poem entitled: "Ten Words With the Power to Help You Walk Away From Useless Suffering."

The "feel" is real,
But the "why" is a lie!

Let this liberating insight into the secret nature of unhappy feelings find a welcome home in you. Dare to apply its wisdom to any moment when some negative state tries to brew up a storm in you, and watch how you can make even the most stubborn sufferings disappear.

REMEMBER THIS SIMPLE TRUTH AND BE SELF-RULING

At this point one great, bright, new idea should be dawning in us: we are not meant to be the slave of any negative thought or feeling, nor are we intended to live under the limitations inherent in these darkened states. Our true role is to be the sovereign governor of our interior lives and all that this spiritual estate implies. It is our spiritual right to decide what kind of thoughts and feelings are permitted to roam through our consciousness and to rule their relationships as the overseer of our own soul. Of this let there be no doubt.

In line with this last idea, the following insight amplifies all our recent lessons regarding learning to let go and live in the Now: *there is not a thought that can stay in our mind, not a feeling that can remain in our heart, that is not willingly remembered.* Let me explain this amazing truth about an equally amazing, but as yet unrealized, power of ours.

Have you ever had appear in your mind the image of someone who hurt you, or run a whole mental movie about something that didn't work out, so that in recalling the event you actually relived the sense of loss? How does such a painful image seem to stay in the mind, especially given the fact of how much we struggle to make it go away? We all know how it feels to try and "fix" such visitations, where we dream up a new solution, tell ourselves what we should have said, hope that something we can think of will make it go away. Of course none of these answers work for one very good reason. Here is the key to unlocking this continuing conflict.

These unwanted images return again and again as they do because something within us keeps recalling them and drawing them to the forefront of our mind. Perhaps your reaction to this lesson is something like: "Impossible! How can that be true since all I want is to free myself of their painful presence?" The answer is self-evident, even though our present senses dictate otherwise.

Since the truth is we do not have to share a single moment with the memory of anything that we don't want to, this means there is something in our present nature that *wants* to recall painful past experiences. Such new self-knowledge lends us the light we need to make higher choices for ourselves, based in conscious awareness. Now we can choose to remember what it is that *we* want to! In other words, rather than allowing ourselves to be drawn into battle with unwanted thoughts or feelings that appear by themselves within our heart and mind, we can do something completely new. We can choose not to focus on what these troubled states want us to; we know that's the road to ruin. Instead we will choose to remember what it is that we want above all else—the Light of Truth that not only reveals what has been hurting us, but that frees us from these unconscious conditions at the same time.

The Wise Ones have always taught the great gift of remembering the Living Light and the practice of placing ourselves in its presence before we embrace anything else. Of course the elevated nature of this kind of remembrance in the face of our trials requires our deliberate and conscious willing of it; but, to paraphrase St. Augustine, "My remembrance of thee is really an effect of thee remembering me." Which means that everything about Reality is already set up to help us succeed with our new aim.

So, in that same moment when you realize that something painful from your past has again pressed its way into you, holding you hostage to a hated image or painful regret, here is what to do: right there, right in that Now, instead of capitulating into that familiar state of feeling yourself to be a captive of what this pain tells you that you must remember (along with all of its suggested solutions for ending the suffering), you choose to remember the Light. Here is a quick look at what this new inner action entails.

Instead of being drawn into a struggle with that unwanted sense of conflict, complete with its cast of supporting characters drawn from your past, intentionally withdraw your attention from that stage show. And at the same time as you close the curtain on it, bring all of your reclaimed attention into the Now. Come awake to the sense of your own physical body. Observe what thoughts and feelings are pressing themselves into your awareness and, while working in the Now like this, welcome into you a conscious remembrance of the Light, of God's Life, of the whole truth as best you understand it.

For instance you might work to remember that the Living Light that has no burden, as opposed to identifying with an old bitterness that is itself the burden that it always blames on others. The key, regardless of one's individual approach, is to make interior effort based upon bringing your new self-knowledge into a willing watchfulness. To help get you started, here are a few other suggestions. When an angry thought flashes in your mind, accompanied by the fiery sensations born of recalling some injustice done to you in the past, instead of remembering the resentments this little image stirs in you, turn the tables on it. Bring its little troubled life into your remembrance of that greater presence within you that dwells well beyond its punishing power. Work like this whenever you can and, like a pebble tossed into a deep pond, the ripple effects of that past pain will simply disappear into the healing nature of the Now. Instead of a life of endless resistance, you will learn the timeless secret of how to replace any form of darkness with the Light you have chosen over it.

Choose to remember the Light. Let it fight for you. Not only will this Living Intelligence lift you above the fray of all that should be forgotten, but it also will guide you back home to a timeless place in yourself where the past no longer dwells.

ASK THE MASTERS

QUESTION: Why do we have so little true understanding of ourselves? What is it that keeps us from seeing Reality as it is and prevents us from discovering our True Self?

ANSWER: *Each one of us is made up of ten thousand different and successive states, a scrap-heap of units, a mob of individuals.*

—Plutarch

QUESTION: Is there a way to explain how things get so turned around inside of us, and what we must do if we are really sincere about wanting to let go and live in the Now?

ANSWER: *In an ancient Indian text a conversation is reported between the pupil and death. Death said: 'God made sense turn outward, man therefore looks outward, not into himself. Sometimes a daring man has looked round and found himself. Then he is immortal!' Here is the beginning of the experiment——to separate from useless states and to remember oneself. This is what man, as an experiment, has to do. Otherwise he fails!*

—P. D. Ouspensky

KEY LESSONS IN REVIEW

1. There is nothing in the universe with the power to hold the human mind in painful captivity except for the cage it builds for itself out of its own mistaken thinking.

2. Detect and deliberately drop all fearful thoughts about what may be your future and you release yourself from a present torment whose unseen driving force is, in fact, your own consent to dwell on darkly imagined tomorrows.

3. Remember that all dark thoughts and feelings require our consent to punish us and that these negative states are, in themselves, literally nothing without the powers we grant them. Then, in this same bright moment of recalling the truth of ourselves, we are made the conqueror of what would overcome us!

4. Spiritually speaking, the cost of starting over is not what we pay to achieve some distant desire, but it is in our willingness to let go of—to dare to live without—any desire we may have whose promise of fulfillment drives us to search for it in yet another tomorrow.

5. Once we understand how to use them, life's many unwanted twists and turns are no longer seen as isolated, disjointed experiences under whose yoke we are born to be burdened, but instead are realized as unique opportunities, whose rewards are the lessons that can lead us, if we will follow them, up to and through the successful education of the soul.

CHAPTER NINE

Awaken the Will and Wisdom to Enlighten Your World

More than anything else at this point in our studies together, I want you to know one thing: When it comes to letting go and living in the Now, *no sincere effort goes unrewarded*. In the long run, it is not our ability to succeed with some individual task that determines our spiritual success, but our willingness to learn what is new and true about ourselves. Within each of us dwells a being without bounds, but unless it is explored and exercised wisely we will never know the heights to which we may rise.

Imagine a newly fledged eaglet whose home rests high upon some rocky cliff, and that today it rises for the first time to stand on the edge of its woven-stick nest. Before now, the only world this little creature had ever known was the sheltering safety of its enclosed aerie, but no longer is this true. Standing there, it peers out over an open and seemingly endless new world, and as it does, a silent but unmistakable invitation sounds itself through the eaglet's heart. Its answer to the call of this expanse is instinctive and immediate: It stretches open its white-tipped wings and feels them catch the swirling updrafts that race their way around the mountainside. Slowly, the young bird rises, teetering in the air, even as its talons involuntarily lock onto the sides of its nest, anchoring it there.

For several days this future king of the skies will run through this exercise, exploring its newly found powers and the promise of flight, though it still remains earthbound. And then there comes a moment when—caught between the instinct to be grounded and the wild longing to fly free—it lets go of the only world it ever knew. In that instant, in a certain sense, it is born again and takes its rightful place in the open airs it was created to rule.

With this simple look into what is commonplace in the natural realm, we catch a glimpse of something supernal. We are given a hint of what we must do to enter into the heavens hidden within ourselves.

LET GO AND LIVE THE EXTRAORDINARY LIFE

I can think of no greater encouragement in this life than the self-evident truth that within each of us dwells something Extraordinary. By "Extraordinary" I don't mean any one condition or sensation born of a particularly exciting experience or even the long-awaited realization of some special achievement. The meaning of Extraordinary I wish to convey goes far beyond all such isolated crowning moments. It points not to these individual gifts of life, but to their immutable and inexhaustible source that is the secret center of each of us: a timeless resource open and available to anyone who would seek this Life that sits behind life as we know it. Surely it is the realization of this Extraordinary Life that St. Paul is referring to when he tells the people of Athens: "For in Him do we live, and move, and have our being." (Acts 17:28) Now, with these last ideas in mind, let's approach this whole idea of an Extraordinary Life from a slightly different angle.

All of us, in one way or another, have either touched or been touched by some form of passing greatness. And while there's little doubt about the pleasure inherent in these personal victories, it's equally evident that all of them are missing one essential element: *They lack the power to satisfy our need to know,* directly, *something truly permanent.* We would have to be deeply asleep in this life if we haven't yet seen that even the best of our dreams become as dust in the winds of time. This is why Vernon Howard, a great American philosopher taught, "It is wise to seek immortality, for time defeats all other ambitions."

Everything physical passes. The truth of this statement is inescapable, which means that in spite of the enigma of searching for something permanent in the midst of this temporal life, it is what must be done. And this is what we will do—starting with a quick look into a special insight that we will need to understand to ensure our success. In those grand moments of life—where we are suddenly given a glimpse of something so inspired, loving, strong, timeless, or beautiful that it quiets the mind—we know we stand in the presence of something that represents the potential for us to know a new and higher order of ourselves. But, what we have yet to learn about each of these bright and vital forces active in us, is that our experience of them represents only a brief interlude between that momentarily receptive part of ourselves and the Extraordinary Life from which they radiate. Again, we can illustrate this celestial idea by calling upon an experience common to all of us.

If you have ever walked through a deep wood on a sunlit day and stood in the silent shafts of light that stream down onto the shaded forest floor, then you know, even though these bright beams appear randomly and seem to stand alone, each ray of light comes from a common source: the sun. So it is with these wonderfully timeless qualities we sometimes see shining through our hearts and minds. All of these celestial characteristics are the too-fleeting expression of our own yet-to-be-realized True Nature, an eternal essence whose secret home is the very center of our own soul. The problem is that our realization of this self-liberating truth still exceeds our grasp, which is why we have yet to claim our place in the sun. But if this potential relationship with Real Life *is* true, and we are meant not only to be aware of all things under the sun, but also to know ourselves as a part of the very light that illuminates this kingdom, then we must ask ourselves this question: why are we missing the mark?

The answer we will find is surprising. The only reason we don't see the entrance to the Extraordinary Life is because we don't know where to look. Perhaps this idea could be better stated this way: we are always looking in all the wrong places. This unseen limitation in the way we see our lives is built right into the fabric of our present nature! Let's see if this is true.

The way our present nature looks at life around us—as well as everything appearing to move within it—is through our five senses. This means that as we are, the sum of our relationship with the world is determined by how we see, hear, smell, touch, and taste our surroundings. And this is an important consideration, for through it we can realize something unseen. These natural faculties report to us— in a ceaseless stream of corresponding sensations—that we live apart from the reality they register—so much so that virtually everything we experience about ourselves tells us that we live in a reality that is happening outside of, or exterior to us. The unfortunate result of this obviously incomplete view of life is that instead of realizing the peace and grace inherent in being aware of our undivided relationship with the Extraordinary Life, we are reduced to frantically searching for what must be only the smallest and most temporary fragments of it.

Unseeing as we are at present—meaning that we have yet to realize that our perception of reality is partial at best—we are unable to comprehend that this limited level of consciousness is itself the *actual cause of our unhappiness.* And so it goes; we continue to chase after what amounts to little more than shadows of Real Life. To live like this is like someone who—seeing a priceless pearl in the sand—tries to convince himself that he should be content with just stealing glimpses of its luster instead of walking over, picking up, and possessing the pearl for himself.

How do we regain our relationship with what is real and Now? What must we do to develop a conscious relationship with the Extraordinary Life that lives within us? The exercises about to be introduced will help us make two valuable discoveries at once. First, they will help us to see that our current nature knows only how to seek itself in passing reflections that it sees as being separate, or other than itself. Second, we will find the answer to what we must do to realize the power and the promise of our True Nature.

SEVEN SIMPLE EXERCISES TO
INVITE THE EXTRAORDINARY LIFE

Each one the following inner practices makes it possible for you to reveal and then release what stands between you and your relationship with the Extraordinary Life. To succeed, all you need is an earnest wish to awaken, coupled with a willingness to go to work on yourself. Should you feel yourself starting to sink just thinking about how far removed you are from the Extraordinary Life—that the distance to go is too great to cover—*never mind all that nonsense.* Listen instead to what St. Francis of Assisi would have you know about why your spiritual success is already spoken for: "I *never think upon Eternity without receiving great comfort, for I say to myself: How could my soul grasp the idea of the Everlastingness, if the two were not related in some way?*"

It is up to us whether or not we fulfill the promise of this extraordinary vision, of this can there can be no doubt. Will we spend our lives in mere dreams of winning a limitless life, only to be shaken awake time and time again by what is seen as a rude reality? Or, will we do the inner-work of awakening ourselves from this dream? Choosing the Extraordinary Life begins with our conscious work to realize it, which the following special practices help to ensure.

1. Let Nagging Questions Go Unanswered. In times of stress, learn to listen to what the Extraordinary Life is trying to tell you about your True Nature, instead of searching anxiously for familiar answers to make your stressed-out self feel right again. All fearful, doubt-filled moments are secret reflections of what we have yet to understand about life and ourselves; they are not life's rejection of us or of our wish for happiness. Choose to go consciously quiet whenever there is a riot in you. Refuse to take part in the search to repair what you fear may be coming undone. Let go and watch what happens when you consciously sacrifice the fear-filled self. This new action allows the Extraordinary Life to enter into you, where its presence alone proves that all is well.

2. Don't Make the Rescue Call. In times of anxiety and fear, we almost always call upon someone or something to help us get through our stress. This dependency on others for strength to see us through our trials not only weakens our soul, but it also steals from us the possibility of being educated by the Extraordinary Life, which means we miss two major lessons. First, the crucial insight that all our fears are based upon false evidence that appears real. With this revelation comes our second realization: the same frightened self that seeks rescue secretly confirms its imagined condition as being real each time it cries out for help. Refusing to rescue ourselves from inner states that scare us invites the Extraordinary Life to show us that no such scared self exists that needs saving.

3. Take the Hard Way. Rut and routine are two sides of the same sad street. Repetitive patterns are the well-worn pavement that our

spiritually asleep Self loves to tread while it talks us to death with empty promises of all the extraordinary times just ahead of us. We can learn to do much better than let ourselves be betrayed in this way, but it takes inner work! Instead of caving into the demands of those slipshod parts of ourselves, which are always looking for the easy way out, we must choose in favor of what our false nature wants us to see as being the "hard" way. But it's not. In fact, once we learn that the only real way out of what we would rather avoid *is to go through it*, in that same moment we discover another self-liberating truth: the only thing that's hard on us is when we allow our unenlightened nature to convince us that getting around something is the same as rising above it.

4. Do the Thing You Fear Doing. There is a correct time and place for thinking through practical plans in the ordinary scheme of life's events. But nothing that is founded in thought can serve to reveal the unthinkable plans that the Extraordinary Life holds in store for anyone willing to leap into the moment without a parachute. Never mind those old fears of falling. Just jump! *Being willing to risk failing is a prerequisite for fearless living.* If you take the leap into what you are psychologically afraid of doing, the Extraordinary Life will prove to you that its unshakable ground is everywhere beneath you at all times. Nothing in the world compares with this discovery because, once realized, there's nowhere for you to go but up! A note of caution: taking a spiritual leap is a far different thing from taking a reckless physical risk. Never risk the well-being of your physical body for the sake of a passing thrill; for what is possible to attain with a body, cannot be done without one. The temporary rush of adrenalin has nothing in common with one's awakening to the reality of a timeless, fearless life.

5. Take Time Out from Yourself Every Day. Unseen by the self that walks upon it, thought is a treadmill powered by the movement

of our yesterdays as they produce our tomorrows. This is the real meaning of "doing time." The domain of the Extraordinary Life is timeless. To share its life, we must enter into its world. Here is a good way to begin: as often as can be remembered, choose to break out of that gilded, but self-confining, cage called "thinking about yourself." We live under the power of these unconscious ponderings, for when they turn dark and stormy, it is we who are left out in the cold. Even if we can only collect ourselves to meditate, pray, take a nature walk, or quietly contemplate some higher idea for a few minutes at a time, we must do it anyway. These small windows—opened by our wish and our work to enter into the Extraordinary Life—grant us passage into its timeless domain.

6. Open Yourself to Life. Dare to see and experience yourself as you are without giving names to all of the varied emotional sensations that present themselves before your watchful inner eyes. Allow the meaning of whatever states you see in yourself to reveal their actual nature to you. Resist the temptation to interrupt their upwelling by constantly trying to explain to yourself why you are experiencing what you are. Have no intention toward these thoughts and feelings other than to be open to them and, in doing so, permit them their uninterrupted passage through you. Why open up to life in this way? For one thing, this spiritual practice gives negative states the back door they need to depart! For another, the Extraordinary Life is very possessive. It will not enter any space marked "occupied."

7. Make No Campsites. The Extraordinary Life visits individuals, not groups or organizations. It strengthens the soul willing to be alone for its sake. Keep your distance from people who insist that you believe as they do, who hope to convince you that the reality they have satisfied themselves with should satisfy you as well.

These deceivers want only to keep you in their unreal camp. Never mind who is walking with you and who isn't. Be wary of any campsite—inner or outer—with its bright Welcome Weary Traveler sign. Most of these campers desire your company so that they can forget they are going nowhere. Walk on! Your persistence is an open invitation for the Extraordinary Life to show you the Way back home.

When it comes to exercises such as these, and all of the others discussed throughout our studies together, we should always remember one thing: whenever the inner-going gets tough, which it must if we are to grow, it is far better for us to temporarily fail at becoming what we intend to be, than it is to succeed at remaining who and what we have been. Teddy Roosevelt, the rugged American President who lived over one hundred years ago, must have had these same ideas in mind when he wrote these spiritually stirring words: "It is not the critic who counts . . . The credit belongs to the man who is actually in the arena; whose face is marred by dust and sweat and blood; who strives valiantly; who errs and comes short again and again; who knows the great enthusiasms, the great devotions, and spends himself in a worthy cause; who at best, knows in the end the triumph of high achievement; and who at worst, if he fails, at last fails while daring greatly."

Now let us turn our attention to how each of us may, every day, help to lift, heal, and enlighten the world we share—so that through our individual spiritual efforts we do the work that first transforms our own lives and then the life of our planet itself. Is this vision attainable? Is there such a work we can do with the power to make so vast a difference? As we are about to learn the answer is . . . yes!

START BEING THE LIGHT OF THE WORLD

Every journey of genuine self-discovery, and the subsequent changes this process produces in us, must begin somewhere. We begin this leg of our journey with a great but unrealized truth: *within each of us resides a power that can change the whole world*. It's true; we each have a secret character hidden away in us that is created for just the alchemical purpose of transforming any dark influence into a beneficial force. And yet, as appealing as the idea of such a power may sound to us, to take conscious possession of its strength is not that simple.

Becoming an instrument of this higher power takes more than merely wishing for its entrance into our life. To realize such a viable wisdom requires *action* in the Now. So let us be clear: we are created with everything that we need to transform and transcend the shadows of fear, regrets, and resentments that prowl the corridors of our sleeping consciousness. And when these secret seeds of conflict have been revealed and released, we are as well, for then nothing negative remains within us to goad us into acting against ourselves. Multiply this possibility by billions of beings and gone are the mindless wars and all the selfish acts of socially accepted gluttony.

Perhaps you are wondering, what is this great power entrusted to us by which we may overcome all of our interior adversaries? Here is the answer: *Each of us is created to be the Light of the world*. Within each of us resides a nascent Light born into this world with us. We can think of this as being the Light of higher conscience by whose compassionate intelligence we are empowered to discern what is helpful from what is harmful, to intuitively know the difference between a genuine act of kindness and a kindness done for selfish reasons. By this Light we are able to tell what is true and what is false. When we do our part to live in the awareness of this Light so that its presence becomes an active power within us, then *what is there that can remain with the power to hurt us*? How can any unseen darkness prevail if its character is revealed *before* it begins its punishing action? Just think of such a power and the freedoms it must bear.

Yet, as encouraging as these words are meant to be, here also is a word of caution: We must take care neither to let our own doubts discount such a hope, nor must we assume possession of what we hope for as a foregone conclusion. Such assumptions always lead to defeat and heartache. We must understand this positive power remains but our *potential*, for if this Living Light were already actualized in us, no negative state could dominate us. Their evil effects would already be non-events, which would mean our world would not be the sorry place that it is.

So our first step in learning to be the light of the world must be to increase our awareness of these various forces at work within us, while being careful to neither judge ourselves for what we see, nor accept any of our findings as an inescapable limitation. In fact, rather than identifying with the usual sense of injury that comes with seeing something unwanted in us, and then mindlessly judging ourselves, we will do something totally new. We will use these same discomforts to remind us to direct our attention to that Living Light within us that has the power to make *any* darkness disappear. Even if all we possess is a faint suspicion that we are created to transcend these troubled thoughts and feelings that vex our soul, that's a fine place to start. The important thing is to begin! We must learn to *actualize* this higher life now being visualized through our intuition. There is no other way to turn our own possibility into a real power. One simple example makes this point.

Years ago someone had an insight that common sunlight could be harnessed in a practical way to produce solar-generated energy. Today we have learned how to transform the sun's energy into our helpful and healthful servant. Now we see a new possibility; we want to become conscious partners with the Light that lives within us; we

sense that *its* power is the same as the strength we need to set ourselves free. So then, how do we illuminate our relationships at home,
in our workplace, wherever we are? What must we do to enlighten this
murky world of ours that staggers under the weight of its own shadows? The answer to this question is as surprising as it may be shocking: *we must cease being an unconscious part of its darkness.*

Please don't think this last spiritual injunction is too simple or too
esoteric to be practical. Just the contrary is true: this instruction is
loaded with no-nonsense power that we can learn to put into immediate practice. We need only realize how the universe itself is set up to
help us succeed with our wish to enlighten our world. The following
insights help prove this vital point:

Is there any light anywhere in the universe that isn't a part of all
the light in the universe? If we will only give this last idea a moment's
consideration, the conclusion is evident: indeed, the light *here* is the
light *there* and is, in fact, the light everywhere. Quantum physics cor-
roborates this spiritual axiom. Twenty-first century scientists have at
last realized what the ancient Wise Ones have always professed: the
timeless indivisibility of light.

Along the same lines, is there darkness anywhere in the universe
that is not a part of the darkness everywhere in the universe? Again,
how can this be otherwise? For instance, and right at the heart of our
study, is the dark hatred or fear that consumes a soul in Britain different
in nature from a similar dark state that consumes someone in Brazil,
even though the two are thousands of miles apart? The answer is no;
they are both the same darkness.

Now, I urge you to ponder the significance of this next finding: If
we bring light into any darkness *anywhere,* is not darkness *everywhere*
made less? Mustn't even the littlest bit of light added to even the
greatest darkness leave that same darkness not so impenetrable? The
answer has to be a brilliant *yes*!

Can we see the possibilities before us? Can we see the significance of the choices we make? Is it clear what we are empowered to do? Once we agree to actualize the Living Light, *everything* around us, everything within the sphere of our awareness may be altered in its fundamental makeup. Negating the negative *positively* changes our reality. But let's not get too far ahead of ourselves. First comes the vision; then we must make the specialized interior efforts needed to effect this transformation of life. . . .

We must no longer allow ourselves to identify with any negative state, regardless of *why* that state tells us we must embrace its painful presence. That is to say, we must become as ruthless in detecting and rejecting these dark thoughts and feelings, as they have been ruthless in wrecking our lives. Here is why this instruction is such a spiritual imperative if we wish to know the light life.

Each time we say "I" to what is destructive or corruptive in us, *we actually incorporate and reinforce* that same dark state. What does this mean, to *incorporate* darkness into one's life? It means, literally, that we *embody* it. A brief explanation helps shed light on this esoteric revelation.

Whenever we identify with negative forces, we unknowingly provide them with two conditions they can't have otherwise: First, we give these chaotic states a place to appear within a plane of reality to which they ordinarily have no other access. And second, at the same time, we lend them the vital life energies they must have to sustain their life-draining presence within our psychic system.

What I would have you glean from these insights is this one great lesson in letting go: Without us to supply these negative states with both the vehicle *and* the life force they need to survive, they cannot flourish. Withdraw water from where weeds grow, and they will wither; it's a natural law. So, if we wish to end our relationship with what compromises us, we are required *to do one thing* to the best of our ability: we must no longer lend ourselves to the will of any dark state looking to use us as *its* vehicle.

Whenever we feel some form of negativity brewing in us—*regardless* of the circumstances, which our lower nature tells us justifies this incorporation—we should work to remember and put into practice our new intention. Now that we know the true nature of these negative states, we can choose to incorporate what is light and right *before* we swallow any other suggested considerations offered to us by our own conflicted nature. This means that in moments of trial, our first task is to wake up, become fully aware of ourselves, and then dare to *do the light thing*. Let's look a bit deeper at what's involved in this new interior action.

Rather than our habitual practice of consulting a host of disturbing thoughts about how to get things settled, which is like asking the proverbial fox to guard the chicken coop, we *see* this contradiction and make an entirely new choice. Instead of trying to imagine who or what we need to rescue us, we become aware of those troubled thoughts and feelings that cause us to feel we are in danger. This act of heightened self-awareness brings all that disturbs us into the light to which we have now turned. In other words, instead of unconsciously allowing what is dark to drag us into its conflicted state, we make a conscious choice to bring the whole of our present condition into *the Light of Now*. This one action transforms all that it encompasses in us, and *everything* changes. Our sense of gladness grows, as gradually the light of higher self-awareness does for us what we have not been able to do for ourselves. We are set free.

Remember all we have just discovered here together. Just as turning our face toward the sun ensures that all shadows remain behind us, so is it true that when we welcome the Light into our lives, we give notice to all negative states. Darkness, your days are numbered! We are done with you!

FOUR WAYS TO TEACH THE TRUTHS
THAT TRANSFORM THE WORLD

Part of our work to let go and live in the Light of Now requires new self-knowledge. Consider the following: Our lives are a part of a perpetual and perfect balance whose invisible power governs all things. This idea is as timeless as it is true. The fabric of our universe is a delicate weave of primordial opposites whose ever-changing expression gives rise to existence as we know it. Listen to the wonderful way Ralph Waldo Emerson expresses this vital insight:

> Polarity, or action and reaction, we meet in every part of nature; in darkness and light; in heat and cold; in the ebb and flow of waters; in male and female; in inspiration and expiration, the systole and diastole of the heart; in electricity, galvanism, and chemical affinity. Super-induce magnetism at one end of a needle; the opposite magnetism takes place at the other end. If the south attracts, the north repels. To empty here, you must condense there. An inevitable dualism bisects nature, so that each thing is a half, and suggests another thing to make it whole; as spirit, matter; man, woman; odd, even; subjective, objective; in, out; upper, under; motion, rest; yea, nay. Whilst the world is thus dual, so is every one of its parts. The entire system of things gets represented in every particle.

In this one reflection is found the venerable wisdom behind Taoist teachings, Buddhist doctrine, the eternally turning seasons of the Old Testament's Ecclesiastes, as well as esoteric Christianity. We are given the eyes to see a ceaseless expression of active and passive forces pressing their way into our essence, where they make their passing impressions. Let us look at this last idea regarding the continuous impressions being made upon and within us.

Our lives take place within a never-ending stream of cosmically generated energies that continually permeate and interpenetrate our bodies, physical and subtle alike. Physicists estimate that in the time it took you to read this last sentence some umpteen billions of ghost-like particles passed right through you! Not only do all these phantom forces go unseen by us, but as these energies move through us, they produce a host of corresponding *resonances* within us. As a result of these subtle influences passing through us, we experience a veritable stream of almost imperceptible sensations (and then reactions) to their presence in our psychic system. Any of these sensations that we *do* become conscious of in ourselves is quickly labeled, given a familiar name, according to our conditioning. Here is the reason we need this knowledge regarding the nature of our broader being in the universe: as we begin to see ourselves in the context of a higher reality, we become empowered with a whole new way to relate to our own ever-changing interior states.

Take for instance one unwanted condition common to most of us: the visitation of a feeling that something vital is missing from our lives. Now, because of our new self-knowledge, we have the chance to realize that while this feeling is real, the *why* that we have given ourselves to explain it is now seen to be a lie. When we look closely at our own experience, we can see that there is no answer to solve this mysterious feeling of having a *hole in our soul*. And this brings us to the special lesson for which we have been preparing.

If nothing we have been able to imagine has the power to dissolve this sense of emptiness, then what should we be looking for? Here's a hint: if we can see that our old answers are, at best, incomplete, maybe what we need are whole *new questions* based in our newly enlarged understanding of reality. Here is one of the new questions we must now ask ourselves: What is it within our souls that is *after us*? Don't let this surprising question throw you; in fact, there is much we already know about these *hounds of heaven*, and why it feels like something unseen is always nipping at our heels!

We human beings are born with an indefinable longing to grow beyond ourselves, to penetrate and illuminate the mysterious depths of our own heart. The ideal and pursuit of perfection is literally seeded into our soul; it pervades our very being. Our longing to walk among the stars does not seem out of reach; the wish to be eternal goes with us everywhere. In more down-to-earth terms, if we wish to live without resentments that linger in our hearts and rid ourselves of fear with all of its debilitating limitations. We must shed the skin of our selfishness. We must learn what it means to consciously suffer ourselves without complaint and have compassion even toward those with whom we disagree. If we do this, we would be on our way to being immortals. Christ's admonition, "Be ye gods," rings true in our innermost ear.

But what we have yet to realize is the actual nature of these celestially prompted longings that push us along to fulfill this promise of our higher nature. The truth is that these forces serve us as both a *disturbance* and *an invitation*; they are one and the same, cosmic opposites of a sort that, once realized as such, reveal the path back home to our True Self. A common example will help us understand *how and why* these celestial energies work as they do within us.

Whenever we feel the onset of a thirst, this physical sensation invites us to seek for something that will quench it. Now consider the way that we *thirst* for the truth of ourselves. But this celestial need of ours—in all of its various forms—*never* stops pouring down into us from the heights of our own True Nature. This call to a higher consciousness may be denied, but it can never be driven from our soul. We must ask: what do we possess with the power to answer these invisible promptings from which we cannot escape?

We are created with the capability of realizing the timeless truth of ourselves, which includes being empowered to use—to release or transform—all the conflicting forces that are woven into the path of the upward Way. *Nothing* can stop us from receiving that Niagara Falls of celestial impressions whose light not only serves to reveal the *still in the dark* character of our undeveloped nature, but also pours into us, all that is needed to evolve beyond it. Now all we need is to learn—and practice—the specialized part we must play in our own transformation.

First, in order to rightly receive these vital impressions that are a prerequisite for becoming conscious of the life lessons they bring in their tow, we must learn what it means to be rightly *passive* in the Now. To understand this important spiritual principle, think of what it would mean to receive life without pre-determined demands upon what you will or won't accept as it unfolds. This state of impersonal conscious awareness is referred to in Eastern wisdom traditions as having one's mind polished like a mirror—perfectly passive to all that passes into and through its consciousness, a silent witness to whatever life reveals. This conscious compliance with a broader reality is the first of two vital stages we must actualize within us *if* we would transform both ourselves and the world in which we live.

The second stage needed for our transformation—after the passive ground of us has been seeded with what we have observed within us—requires we become *active*. We have received, now we must *give*. The opposites must be united within us by our own conscious efforts. For instance, say we've worked hard to be more aware of ourselves in the Now, and that for this effort we catch a glimpse of how quick we are to judge others, to criticize them for their "failings." This pain that strains us—and those we touch with it—is itself a creation of a false sense of our own perfection. But our awareness of its punishing presence within us *is the same as our invitation to transcend the negative nature that is responsible for it.* So, if we want to realize the higher level of Self that reveals the need for further transformation, then we have work to do. We must actualize this new level of ourselves by acting from our new understanding in a whole different way.

In each instance where we see that we still have more to understand about ourselves, we must use our lives to become a living example of those qualities of character that we need to learn. In other words, in order to transcend what we have seen as limiting us, we must teach, by example, what we would further understand. In a moment, I will set out some very clear examples of this kind of conscious action, but for now—if we wish to realize the Extraordinary Life—let us see why our wish requires such work from us.

Until we realize that all the influences that act upon us and set the stage for our various life lessons are really just secret reflections of some undetected imbalance in us, which are asking for correction, none of these impressions can be truly received, nor the lessons behind them rightfully learned. These wide ranging inner impressions, along with the often-challenging life lessons that appear with them, are not created to punish us. They exist to help temper our soul's character, to help us learn to integrate the many conflicting opposites within us. In each instance we emerge from one order of Self into a new nature, whose being is greater than the sum of those unconscious tendencies now united within it.

So you see, it is not enough to just passively receive these special lessons. We must act upon their revelations and further clarify their import. This is why our willingness *to teach* for the purpose of learning is every bit as important as is our willingness to learn what we must in order to grow.

Following are four ways to teach the truths that transform the world we live in, even as we ourselves are transformed by our own actions. It is vital for us to remember that these suggested practices are designed to help us achieve an enhanced spiritual balance in ourselves, even as, through these same actions, we teach others around us about the possibility of living from a whole new order of self-understanding.

1.   We teach others when we do not react in alarm to some potentially frightening news or event. The world around us receives the lesson that those events —in themselves—do not have the power to make or break the awakened soul. Our lesson—if we will teach it—is to see that we need not ride along on own three-alarm nature that loves getting set off.

2.   We teach others when they can see us laugh at our own mistakes. The world around us receives the lesson that there is a big difference between making a mistake and thinking of oneself as being a mistake. Our lesson—if we will teach it—is to see that any compulsive wish to be seen as perfect in the eyes of the world is a punishment that can never be a part of our true peace and contentment.

3.   We teach others around us when we won't give voice to complaint. The world around us receives the lesson that there are superior ways to handle times of discomfort or disappointment that do not include expressing negative emotions. Our lesson—if we will teach it—is to see that we can use passing dark states to awaken to and realize an interior wisdom that knows how to use everything for its own growth.

4.   We teach others whenever we refuse to psychologically defend ourselves—be this against simple sarcasm or even vicious slander. The world around us receives the lesson that what is true needs no defense and that what is false cannot be defended. Our lesson—if we will teach it—is the realization that people only feel the need to attack what frightens them and that we need never live in fear of any frightened person.

Our real spiritual development is under invisible laws: To grow, we must learn. To learn, we must teach. To teach we must lead. To lead, we must make mistakes. Making mistakes tills the ground of us, making it receptive to new and higher lessons, and thus the positive spiral completes itself, even as it rises above its original starting point.

Take these suggested exercises and work with them to teach the truths that transform the world around and within you. Make up your own exercises based on the lessons you know that life is asking you to learn. Always strive to remember, according to the principles we have learned throughout this book, that anything we work to change in ourselves cannot help but change *everything*. What can be more promising than that?

ASK THE MASTERS

QUESTION: I don't know about others, but I have thought about these questions for some time now and, try as I might, I can't seem to get beyond myself. What am I missing?

ANSWER: *For the powers of our mind, life and body are bound to their own limitations and however high they may rise or however widely expand, they cannot rise beyond them. But still, mental man can open to what is beyond him and call down a Supramental Light, Truth, and Power to work in him and do what the mind cannot do. If mind cannot by effort become what is beyond mind, Supermind can descend and transform mind into its own substance.* —Sri Aurobindo

QUESTION: I have the wish to awaken and to know my own True Nature, but how can I know if I am suited for such a journey?

ANSWER: *Like the fish, swimming in the vast sea and resting in its deeps, and like the bird, boldly mounting high in the sky, so the soul feels its spirit moving through the vastness and the depth and the unutterable richness of love . . . and then love makes the soul so bold that it no longer fears man or friend, angel or saint or God Himself in all that it does or abandons, in all its work-ing or resting.* —Bd. Beatrice of Nazareth

KEY LESSONS IN REVIEW

1. Every conscious act of love lifts the world so that each genuine expression of kindness embraces and elevates all willing souls. Every angry thought lashes the soul, infecting the world with its bitterness until the will of what is dark within that hatefulness, crushes the unwitting soul, causing her to lose her precious little light.

2. Every moment that unfolds in life presents us with an invitation to choose either the path of what will better us—as when we choose conscious kindness over unthinking cruelty or a path that will embitter us—as when we unconsciously embrace a resentment instead of working to release it. To be wise is to choose in favor of the Better Path, even though the bitter one often seems the easier.

3. Here is how to receive a gift from life greater than can be told: never again give to another person any thought or feeling that you wouldn't want to keep for yourself.

4. Learning to be grateful for the lessons hard learned is the secret and greater lesson hidden within all moments of the soul's education.

5. The seed of greatness is sown in an instant, but, in this world of ours, everything great takes time to grow. This means that patience, mingled with persistence, is the special nutriment that sustains all things great. Therefore, should we wish to win the Great Life, we need only add equal measures of quiet watchfulness to our spiritual willingness and a Great Goodness cannot help but flourish within us.

CLOSING WORDS:
THE ROAD TO SELF-REALIZATION

There is one last bit of writing I would leave with you before we part ways, for now, on the path to self-realization. Anyone can spy a bright mountaintop and even see some of its wonders from where they stand safely beneath it. Only the few want to breathe the rarified air found at its summit; only the few will take the road that leads to the base of that mountain and gird themselves there for the climb of their life. For those of you who would learn to let go and live in the Now, consider my closing words to be more than just a conclusion to our journey together; They are intended to impart three things at once: invitation, instruction, and spiritual imperative. Please welcome them into your heart.

Some take the high road.
Some take the low road.
Some take the road with friends and family.
Others take it alone.

Some travel with clowns and animals.
Some take only walking shoes.

Some take the road with guru and saint,
While others take the road with drunks.

Some walk the road so slowly as to stand still,
Even as some sprint toward a finish line as if it's in sight.
Some take the road filled with dreams.
Others take the road to leave their dreams behind.

Some take the road and wait for each sunrise,
While others walk all night, every night.
Some don't want to take the road at all
But wind up taking it anyway . . .
While others say they take the road,
But only walk when they can stay in one place no longer.

Some take the road with a forced smile.
Some dampen the road with their tears.
Some take the road and kick up dust with dancing heels
Just happy to be upon it wherever it goes!
Some take the road and pray the entire way,
While others sing to fill the emptiness that comes each
    time
They round a bend and see only more road ahead.

Some take the road and help others along the way,
While others can't help themselves from wishing
They were ahead of everyone walking just ahead of them.
Some take the road and complain the whole way.

Some take the road with sheer gratitude that they can still walk.

The point is *it does not matter how you take the road* . . .

All that really matters is that *you take it.*

BIBLIOGRAPHY

Allen, James. *As a Man Thinketh*. Sante Fe: Sun Books, 1983.

Bennett, J.G. *Deeper Man*. Santa Fe: Bennett Books, 1994.

Bloom, Harold and Marvin Meyer. *The Gospel of St. Thomas*. San Francisco: HarperSanFrancisco, 1992.

Bucke, Richard Maurice. *Cosmic Consciousness*. New York: Penguin Books, 1969.

Bullett, Gerald. *The Testament of Light*. Avenel, NJ: Wings Books, 1994.

Clement, Oliver. *The Roots of Christian Mysticism*. New York: New City Press, 1995.

Saint Augustine and R.S. Pine-Coffin. *Confessions*. New York: Dorset Press, 1986.

Collin, Rodney. *The Mirror of Light*. Boston: Shambhala, 1959.

Eckhart, Meister. *The Man from Whom God Hid Nothing*. Boston: Shambhala, 1996.

Emerson, Ralph Waldo. *Selected Essays of Ralph Waldo Emerson*. New York: Penguin Books, 1984.

Gilbert, Mark. *Wisdom of the Ages*. Garden City, NY: Garden City Publications, 1936.

Gurdjieff, G.I. *Meetings with Remarkable Men*. New York: E.P. Dutton & Co., 1969.

Guyon, Jeanne. *Genesis*. Auburn, ME: Christian Books, 1972.

Hartman, Franz. *Jacob Boehme: Life and Doctrines*. Blauvelt, NY: Steiner Books, 1977.

The Holy Bible: King James Version. New York: Cambridge University Press, 1980.

Howard, Vernon. *The Mystic Masters Speak*. Boulder City, NV: New Life Books, 1974.

————. *The Power of Your Supermind*. Englewood Cliffs, NJ: Prentice Hall, 1988.

James, William. *The Varieties of Religious Experience*. New York: Penguin Books, 1982.

Krishnamurti, J. *Early Writings, Vol. 7*. Bombay, India: Chetana, 1971

————. *The Flame of Attention*. San Francisco: Harper & Row, 1984.

Leary, William. *The Hidden Bible*. New York: C&R Anthony, Inc., 1952.

Watson, Lillian. *Light From Many Lamps*. New York: Simon and Schuster, 1951.

Mood, John, L. *Rilke on Love and Other Difficulties*. New York: WW Norton & Co. 1995.

Nicoll, Maurice. *Psychological Commentaries on the Teachings of Gurdjieff & Ouspensky*. York Beach, ME: Samuel Weiser, 1980.

Nicoll, Maurice. *The New Man*. Utrecht, the Netherlands: Eureka Edition, 1999.

Morris, Audrey Stone. *One Thousand Inspirational Things*. New York: Hawthorne Books, 1951.

Ouspensky, P.D. *In Search of the Miraculous*. New York: Harvest/HBJ Books, 1976.

————. *The Fourth Way*. New York: Vintage Books, 1971.

Schimmel, Annemarie. *I Am Light, You Are Fire: The Life and Works of Rumi*. New York: WW Norton, 1975.

The Song of Solomon. Philadelphia: Running Press, 1990.

Thoreau, Henry David. *Walden*. Boston: Shambhala, 1992.

Tozer, A.W. *Men Who Met God*. Camp Hill, PA: Christian Publications, 1986.

Underhill, Evelyn. *Mystics of the Church*. Harrisburg, PA: Morehouse Publications, 1995.

Wright, Louis B. and Virginia A LaMar. *The Play's the Thing*. New York: Harper & Row, 1963.

ABOUT THE AUTHOR

 Guy Finley's encouraging and accessible message is one of the true bright lights in our world today. His ideas cut straight to the heart of our most pressing personal and social issues—relationships, fear, addiction, stress and anxiety, peace, happiness, freedom—and lead the way to a higher life.

Director of the nonprofit Life of Learning Foundation, Guy is the author of over twenty-five books and audio albums that have sold over a million copies in twelve languages worldwide. His most popular titles include *Apprentice of the Heart*, *The Secret of Letting Go*, *Education of the Soul*, *Lost Secrets of Prayer*, *Design Your Destiny*, and *Seeker's Guide to Self-Freedom*.

In addition, Guy has presented over one thousand unique self-realization seminars to thousands of grateful students throughout North America and Europe over the past twenty years. He has been a guest on hundreds of television and radio shows, including national appearances on ABC, NBC, CBS, CNN, NPR, and many others. He also hosts his own weekly radio and television shows on the Wisdom Network.

Guy Finley lives and teaches in southern Oregon. If you would like to write to him about this book, receive information about his ongoing classes, or request a catalog of his works (along with a free helpful study guide), send a self-addressed, stamped envelope to:

Guy Finley
Life of Learning Foundation
P.O. Box 10-N
Merlin, OR 97532
Office: 541.476.1200 Fax 541.472.0822

FREE GIFTS FOR YOU

For a complete list of over one hundred life-healing works by Guy Finley, visit his award-winning, multimedia website at *www.guyfinley.com*. Browse through all of the free resource materials and read or listen to excerpts from selected books and tapes. Request a free poster filled with helpful guidance and join the foundation's free Key Lesson Club. Each week you'll receive an encouraging inner-life insight delivered right to your desktop via e-mail.

THE LIFE OF
LEARNING FOUNDATION

Life of Learning is a nonprofit organization founded by author Guy Finley in 1992. Its foremost purpose is to help individuals realize their true relationship with life through higher self-studies. The foundation is operated and run solely by volunteers. Everyone is welcome.

Guy Finley speaks four times each week at the foundation to the men and women who gather there to learn more about self-realization. Everyone is invited to come and share in the powerful transformational atmosphere that permeates each insight-filled talk. Each meeting awakens new energies, deepens intuitive powers, heals past hurts, and delivers welcome relief.

Life of Learning rests in the heart of southern Oregon's most beautiful country, upon fourteen acres of old-growth sugar pine. Visitors enjoy the beautiful flower gardens, organic foods, and walking trails with special places for meditation along the way. Twice a year the foundation hosts special retreats for out-of-state students during the third weeks of December and June. The "Talks in the Pines" are an annual favorite.

Whether you enjoy its wild rivers, scenic lakes, old-growth forests, mountain hiking, or strolling along the rugged Pacific Coast, when you visit Life of Learning you're only minutes away from Nature at her best. Life of Learning is located in the community of Merlin, Oregon. Just seven miles away is the city of Grants Pass. Visit *www.guyfinley.com* and request a visitor's pamphlet for a list of local accommodations.

PRAISE FOR GUY FINLEY'S PREVIOUS WORK

"Guy Finley's books are essential guides for positive living and achieving your maximum potential."
—Suzanne Somers, actress

"Guy Finley doesn't just talk about self-freedom but leads you through the doors of yourself into a Higher World within yourself where you discover you are already free!"
—Alan Corbeth, Executive Producer,
Coast to Coast with Art Bell

"Guy takes the wisdom of the ages and uses it to gently coax you to heal the places in your mind where psychological problems originate. The Secret of Letting Go is not an empty promise. It's the key to self-transformation—to an effortless new life. Enjoy the journey."
—Desi Arnaz, Jr., actor

"Guy's teachings are at the top of the 'mountain' of self-transformation tools. Thanks you, Guy, for making what is made complex simple and practical. But, most importantly, real and lasting!"
—Vince McConnell, Eternally Transformed Enterprises

"One of the leading experts at the forefront of human potential."
—Nightingale-Conant

TO OUR READERS

Red Wheel, an imprint of Red Wheel/Weiser, publishes books on topics ranging from spunky self-help, spirituality, personal growth, and relationships to women's issues and social issues. Our mission is to publish quality books that will make a difference in people's lives—how we feel about ourselves and how we relate to one another and to the world at large. We value integrity, compassion, and receptivity, both in the books we publish and in the way we do business.

Our readers are our most important resource, and we value your input, suggestions, and ideas about what you would like to see published. Please feel free to contact us, to request our latest book catalog, or to be added to our mailing list.

Red Wheel/Weiser, LLC
P.O. Box 612
York Beach, ME 03910-0612
www.redwheelweiser.com